Loving Someone with Autism and Complex PTSD

A Partner's Guide to Meltdowns, Shutdowns, Trauma Flashbacks, Real Safety, and Staying Connected Without Losing Yourself

Llewellyn Wesley Doyle

This book is provided for general educational and informational purposes. It is not a substitute for individual medical care, mental health assessment, diagnosis, psychotherapy, couples therapy, crisis intervention, or advice from a qualified professional. The material is intended to help readers think more clearly about relationship patterns and possible responses, not to diagnose another person or determine the cause of behaviour from outward signs alone.

No particular personal, clinical, or relationship result is promised. Readers remain responsible for their own decisions, boundaries, safety, and use of the information presented. Where there is violence, coercion, threats, danger, or concern for immediate safety, appropriate professional or emergency assistance should be sought.

Unless specifically identified otherwise, names, examples, conversations, and scenarios used for teaching purposes are fictional, composite, or altered to illustrate common situations. They are not intended to identify, harm, accuse, imitate, or misrepresent any individual, organisation, clinician, or other entity.

First Edition;2026

ISBN 979-8-90678-206-9

Staten House

Table of Contents

Preface

Autism and traumatic stress are often discussed in separate bodies of books, clinical guidance, and public education. That separation can become unhelpful inside a close relationship, because the same person may be autistic and also carry the effects of repeated trauma. Sensory overload can affect communication, speech, responsiveness, and tolerance for touch or additional input, while trauma can bring re-experiencing, avoidance, heightened threat responses, and changes in emotional and relational functioning. A partner may therefore know a great deal about autism or trauma and still be uncertain about what a particular moment calls for.

This book uses the term Complex PTSD in line with the ICD-11 model, which includes the core features of PTSD together with persistent difficulties involving emotion regulation, self-concept, and relationship functioning. Autism is not treated here as a trauma response, and trauma is not treated as an explanation for autism. They are different conditions with different histories, yet they can affect the same person's capacity, communication, sensory tolerance, threat response, and recovery needs. The practical problem is therefore not simply identifying which label belongs to which behaviour. It is deciding how to respond when the cause is uncertain or mixed.

That is the gap this book addresses. Partners are often told to communicate clearly, reduce sensory pressure, offer reassurance, use grounding, give space, set boundaries, and avoid escalating conflict. All of that advice can be sensible in the right context. The difficulty is timing. A person in sensory overload may need fewer words and reduced input. Autism guidance specifically recommends creating quiet space, reducing stimulation, and allowing recovery time during overwhelm. Someone in shutdown may temporarily have little speech available, while the relationship issue that preceded the shutdown may still require a later answer. When several processes are active at once, certainty may not be possible.

The central framework of this book is the **Moment Map**. It is not a diagnostic instrument. It is a response-selection model built around four working states: meltdown, shutdown, trauma flashback, and mixed or unclear dysregulation. Each state is paired with a practical protocol. Across all four protocols, the same principles remain steady: protect safety, lower unnecessary demand, respect consent, observe what is happening, and return to accountability when capacity has recovered. The aim is to help partners make a safer next choice without asking them to become clinicians.

This book also extends the partner-facing focus of *Loving Someone with Complex PTSD* by addressing a second question that trauma-only guidance cannot answer well enough: what changes when the person who carries trauma is also autistic? The answer affects sensory needs, communication timing, expectations around speech, recovery from overload, and the form that support may need to take.

The primary audience is the spouse or romantic partner of an autistic adult who has Complex PTSD, PTSD, or strong trauma symptoms, especially where one or both conditions were identified in adulthood. Adult children, close family members, and therapists may also find the framework useful. This book does not diagnose, replace therapy, guarantee relationship outcomes, or ask a partner to tolerate intimidation, violence, coercion, or repeated harm. It offers education, practical tools, and a structure for making more informed decisions while preserving the wellbeing and responsibility of both people.

Its purpose is simple: **to help you work out what this moment may need, respond with care, and return to the relationship without losing yourself.**

Reader Note

This book is educational. It is not a diagnostic manual, a substitute for individual medical or psychological care, or a way to determine another person's diagnosis from behaviour you can observe at home. Autism, post-traumatic stress disorder (PTSD), and complex post-traumatic stress disorder (CPTSD) require professional assessment when diagnosis is needed. CPTSD is a distinct diagnosis in ICD-11; diagnostic systems differ across countries and settings (World Health Organization [WHO], 2024a).

The practical framework in this book has a narrower purpose: to help partners choose a safer, lower-pressure response when an autistic person who also carries trauma becomes highly dysregulated. Sometimes you will know what is happening. Sometimes you will only have clues. The goal is not perfect certainty. The goal is to reduce harm, protect both people, and postpone problem-solving until enough capacity has returned.

If anyone is in immediate danger, if there is violence, if someone is unable to remain safe, or if a medical emergency may be occurring, safety takes priority over every communication technique in this book. Leave the immediate situation when necessary and contact appropriate local emergency or professional services.

The fictional examples in this book are composites created for teaching. They do not describe real individuals.

How to Use This Book

You can read the book in order, and there is a reason to do so. The first chapters build the distinctions that make the later protocols easier to use. But this is also a book for the moment after a door closes, a voice rises, a body goes still, or a conversation suddenly becomes impossible. For that reason, the five tools in the next section come before Chapter 1.

Read them now. Return to them often. Mark the pages. Copy the one-page versions into your phone. Rewrite the wording with your partner when both of you are calm. A protocol written by one person about another is only a starting point. A protocol built together becomes part of the relationship.

The five tools are:

1. The Moment Map.

2. The Meltdown Protocol.
3. The Shutdown Protocol.
4. The Flashback Protocol.
5. The Mixed/Unclear Protocol.

These tools share one rule: **state before story**. When a nervous system is overwhelmed or experiencing the past as present, the content of the argument is rarely the first problem to solve. First work out what level of safety, input, orientation, and space the moment can tolerate. The story can be discussed later.

The Core System

Asset 1: The Moment Map

The Moment Map is a response-selection tool. It is not a diagnostic test.

Imagine four destinations on a simple map:

- **Meltdown:** overload is moving outward.
- **Shutdown:** overload is moving inward.
- **Trauma flashback or trauma activation:** the nervous system is responding as though danger from the past is present now.
- **Mixed/unclear:** more than one process may be active, or there is not enough information to tell.

The map begins with four questions.

Question 1: Is anyone unsafe?

Before you interpret behaviour, check the physical situation.

Ask yourself:

- Is anyone being hit, restrained, threatened, cornered, or prevented from leaving?
- Are objects being thrown or broken in a way that could injure someone?
- Is there driving, self-harm, substance use, or access to a weapon creating immediate danger?
- Is there a medical concern such as fainting, breathing difficulty, injury, severe confusion, or a new neurological symptom?
- Are children or other vulnerable people present?

If the answer is yes, move to safety. Do not stay in danger to prove that you understand autism or trauma. A diagnosis may explain vulnerability to dysregulation; it does not make another person's body, property, freedom, or fear irrelevant.

Question 2: What was building before this moment?

Look backward before you look inward.

A meltdown or shutdown often follows cumulative load: noise, light, social performance, change, pain, hunger, fatigue, too many decisions, interrupted routines, conflict, masking, work demands, or a long day with no recovery space. The final event may be small because it is the last addition to a system that was already full. Autistic people themselves have described burnout as chronic exhaustion, loss of skills, and reduced tolerance to stimulus, which can reduce the buffer available for ordinary demands (Raymaker et al., 2020).

A trauma flashback may follow a reminder with a connection to earlier threat: a tone of voice, smell, date, room, sexual situation, door movement, criticism, facial expression, argument pattern, financial conflict, bodily sensation, or feeling of being trapped. The reminder may make sense immediately, or it may not be obvious to either partner.

Do not treat the trigger as a courtroom exhibit. You are looking for context, not proof.

Question 3: Where is capacity moving?

Now watch what is changing.

Outward movement can include shouting, crying, pacing, repetitive speech, frantic movement, pushing away input, intense stimming, or a visible loss of behavioural control. That pattern may point toward meltdown, especially when it follows cumulative overload.

Inward movement can include silence, loss or reduction of speech, stillness, curling up, hiding, retreating, delayed responses, inability to choose, or reduced engagement. That pattern may point toward shutdown.

Past-into-present movement can include reacting to something that is not happening now, appearing to relive or re-experience a traumatic event, sudden terror linked to a reminder, statements that suggest the current partner has become fused with a past threat, or an urgent need to escape despite present safety. PTSD flashbacks can involve a sense that the traumatic event is happening again; grounding strategies aim to reconnect the person with the current time and place (U.S. Department of Veterans Affairs [VA], n.d.-a).

None of these signs is exclusive. A person can become quiet in trauma. A person can shout during a flashback. A trauma reminder can push an already overloaded autistic person into meltdown. That is why the fourth destination exists.

Question 4: What lowers distress without increasing danger?

The response is also information.

Does the person settle when sensory and verbal input are reduced? That supports an overload formulation.

Does calm orientation to the present help? That may support trauma activation.

Does talking itself increase distress? Reduce language.

Does being left completely alone increase panic? Offer quiet presence without demands.

Does touch cause flinching or escalation? Stop touching.

Does a familiar weighted blanket, dark room, rocking movement, shower, headphones, floor position, or repetitive activity help? Make access easier if it is safe.

The point is not to conduct experiments on your partner. The point is to notice what the nervous system is already telling you.

The Moment Map in One Sentence

> **Check safety, notice what built up, watch where capacity is moving, and choose the lowest-risk response that reduces pressure.**

What the Moment Map Does Not Tell You

It does not tell you whether a hurtful statement was acceptable.

It does not tell you whether the relationship is healthy.

It does not tell you whether a partner is responsible for repair.

It does not tell you whether someone has PTSD, CPTSD, dissociation, depression, panic disorder, or another condition.

It answers only the first question: **What does this moment need before we try to solve anything else?**

Asset 2: The Meltdown Protocol

A meltdown is best understood as a loss of behavioural control under overwhelm, not as a deliberate performance designed to win an argument. Public autism guidance describes meltdowns as responses to overwhelming sensory or emotional load and recommends reducing input, staying calm, giving time, and allowing recovery (National Autistic Society, 2020; Leicestershire Partnership NHS Trust, n.d.).

The protocol is:

1. Protect safety without turning safety into punishment

Move breakable or dangerous objects if you can do so safely. Give physical distance. Keep exits available. Move children away from a dangerous scene. Do not crowd the person, block the doorway, restrain them unless an immediate emergency and appropriate professional guidance make that unavoidable, or stand over them demanding control.

If the behaviour becomes violent or threatening, leave when you can do so safely. Understanding overload does not require remaining within reach of harm.

2. Reduce input

Turn down lights. Reduce noise. Stop multiple people from talking. Close a door if the person wants it. Pause television, music, or notifications. Move out of a crowded space. Offer access to headphones, sunglasses, a familiar room, or another known regulating support.

Think subtraction before addition.

3. Use fewer words

During intense overload, language can become another demand.

Prefer:

- "I'm here."
- "You don't need to answer."
- "The room is clear."
- "I'm moving back."
- "Water is on the table."

- "We can talk later."

Avoid speeches, explanations, repeated questions, moral arguments, and "calm down."

4. Stop solving the conflict

Do not continue proving your point because the facts are important. The facts may still matter. They can wait.

A useful sentence is: **"We are not deciding this now."**

That sentence protects both people. It means the issue is postponed, not erased.

5. Treat touch as a question, not a default

Some people seek deep pressure or firm contact during overload. Others cannot tolerate touch at all. Trauma can make touch more complicated. Use prior agreements where possible. In the moment, ask only if the person can process the question. If they pull away, freeze, flinch, or say no, stop.

6. Allow the body to come down

Crying, rocking, pacing, repetitive movement, lying on the floor, covering the ears, retreating under bedding, or silence may be part of recovery for some people. Do not demand a quick return to normal appearance.

7. Delay the debrief

Do not ask, "Why did you do that?" five minutes after the peak.

Recovery may require quiet, food, hydration, sleep, familiar activity, low light, or solitude. The review belongs to a later phase.

8. Return to accountability after capacity returns

Meltdown is not a waiver for harm. If someone screamed insults, broke property, frightened children, drove dangerously, or injured another person, the event must still be addressed. The difference is timing. First restore safety and capacity. Later discuss impact, responsibility, repair, prevention, and professional help when needed.

Meltdown Protocol: Pocket Version

Safety. Subtract input. Fewer words. No debate. Touch only by consent. Allow recovery. Review later.

Asset 3: The Shutdown Protocol

Shutdown can look deceptively calm. From the outside, a person may be silent and still while internally they are using almost all available capacity simply to remain present.

NHS-linked autism guidance describes shutdown as a response to overwhelm in which communication and engagement can reduce sharply (Leicestershire Partnership NHS Trust, n.d.). The partner's task is not to extract speech. It is to reduce demand while preserving a clear path back to connection.

1. Check safety and basic responsiveness

If the behaviour is completely new, unusually severe, involves loss of consciousness, injury, inability to breathe normally, or other medical concern, do not assume autism. Seek medical assessment.

If this is a familiar shutdown pattern and immediate safety is intact, lower demands.

2. Stop requiring normal conversation

Do not ask ten versions of the same question.

Instead of:

"What's wrong? Are you angry? Did I do something? Why won't you answer? Can you at least tell me if we're okay?"

try:

> **"You don't have to talk. I will give you space. You can text me or use the card when you're able."**

3. Offer lower-bandwidth communication

Depending on the person, options may include:

- yes/no questions;
- thumbs up/down;
- pointing;
- a traffic-light card;
- text message while in the same house;
- selecting from two choices;

- a pre-agreed phrase such as "offline, not leaving."

Do not turn an accommodation into another test. If even a yes/no question is too much, stop asking.

4. Reduce sensory and social demand

Quiet the environment. Reduce eye-contact expectations. Do not hover. Give physical space. Remove unnecessary decisions. Make water, food, medication, blankets, or familiar sensory supports accessible without repeated prompting.

5. Protect the relationship from ambiguous silence

A shutdown can be painful for the other partner, especially if silence resembles past abandonment, punishment, or stonewalling. That pain matters.

The solution is not to force speech from a person who cannot currently produce it. The solution is a pre-agreed **return signal**.

Examples:

- "I am shut down. I am not ending the relationship."
- "I need three hours. I will text by 8 p.m."
- "No words. Safe. Talk tomorrow."

The signal can be printed on a card if speech disappears.

6. Do not confuse capacity with accountability

A person can be unable to talk now and still be responsible for returning to the issue later.

This distinction is one of the most important in the book:

> **No capacity now does not mean no responsibility later.**

If difficult subjects are repeatedly followed by silence that is never revisited, the couple has a relationship problem even if shutdown is genuine. The answer is not forcing discussion during shutdown. It is creating a reliable re-entry process afterward.

7. Re-enter slowly

When speech returns, do not immediately unload everything that accumulated while the person was quiet. Begin with orientation:

- "Are you ready for words?"
- "Do you want ten minutes or tomorrow?"
- "Would text be easier?"

Then discuss one issue at a time.

Shutdown Protocol: Pocket Version

> **Safety. Stop demanding speech. Lower bandwidth. Lower sensory load. Use a return signal. Re-enter later.**

Asset 4: The Flashback Protocol

A trauma flashback is not simply remembering something upsetting. PTSD involves re-experiencing, avoidance, and a persistent sense of current threat; flashbacks can involve feeling as if the traumatic event is happening again (WHO, 2024b; VA, n.d.-a).

The partner's role is not to conduct trauma processing. It is to support present-time safety and, when welcomed, grounding.

1. Confirm present safety

Remove current threats where possible. Stop the argument. Increase distance if closeness is being experienced as dangerous. Keep exits open. Do not corner the person to prove that you are safe.

2. Orient gently to the present

Use calm, concrete statements:

- “You are in our bedroom.”
- “It is Tuesday evening.”
- “I am Arden, not him.”
- “The door is open.”
- “You can leave the room.”
- “You are not trapped here.”

The VA's National Center for PTSD recommends grounding through noticing where you are, reminding yourself of the current year and safety, moving, drinking water, and connecting with trusted support (VA, n.d.-a).

3. Offer grounding; do not impose it

Many popular grounding techniques rely on sensory input. That can be useful for some autistic people and intolerable for others. A bright light, cold object, strong smell, unexpected touch, or demand to list five things may increase overload.

Ask beforehand, when calm: **“What helps you know you are here?”**

Possible answers might include:

- seeing a specific object in the room;
- reading a card with the date and address;

- feeling feet on the floor;
- holding a familiar fabric;
- listening to one known voice;
- looking at a pet;
- slow repetitive movement;
- stepping outside;
- naming the current day and planned activity.

The correct grounding method is the one the person can tolerate and has chosen.

4. Keep your language factual

Avoid arguing with fear.

Instead of “That's ridiculous; I would never hurt you,” try: **“I can see you are frightened. I am standing by the door. I will not touch you.”**

Instead of “You're safe, you're safe, you're safe” repeated rapidly, give one concrete cue and reduce pressure.

5. Do not demand the trauma story

Do not ask for details of what happened in the past. Do not press for names, dates, memories, or explanations while the person is activated. Trauma-focused treatment belongs with qualified clinicians and should be adapted to the individual's needs; evidence-based PTSD therapies include trauma-focused approaches such as CPT, PE, and EMDR, while work on autistic clients points to the importance of autism-informed adaptation (VA, n.d.-b; Fisher et al., 2023).

6. Respect touch boundaries

A hug can be soothing to one person and terrifying to another. Never use surprise touch as a grounding technique for someone with a trauma history unless that has been clearly requested and remains welcome.

7. Afterward, separate the reminder from the relationship issue

If a real disagreement triggered a flashback, both things can be true:

- the trauma response deserves care;
- the original disagreement may still require discussion.

Do not use trauma activation to erase the content forever. Do not use the content to deny the trauma response.

Flashback Protocol: Pocket Version

Safety. Stop the conflict. Orient to now. Offer chosen grounding. Do not interrogate memory. No surprise touch. Return to the issue later.

Asset 5: The Mixed/Unclear Protocol

This is the protocol you may use most often.

Research increasingly documents the need to understand trauma in autistic people without assuming that every symptom belongs neatly to one condition. Autistic adults report high levels of trauma exposure and PTSD symptoms, and researchers have warned about diagnostic overshadowing, in which trauma-related changes are mistaken for autism-related features (Andrzejewski et al., 2024; Kildahl & Helverschou, 2024).

In ordinary relationships, the overlap is even harder to sort in real time. A loud argument may be a trauma reminder. The argument may also add enough sensory and emotional load to trigger meltdown. A person may begin in flashback and end in shutdown. An autistic person in burnout may have almost no spare capacity for either sensory demand or trauma reminders.

When you do not know, use the common denominator.

1. Safety first

Move away from danger. Keep exits open. Reduce the audience. Protect children. Do not restrain, block, or corner.

2. Stop adding demand

Pause the argument. Stop asking for explanations. Reduce choices. Use fewer words.

3. Reduce sensory load

Lower noise, light, motion, and social input where possible.

4. Add only gentle present-time orientation

One or two factual cues can help without turning the moment into a trauma exercise:

> **"We are at home. The argument is paused. You do not have to answer me."**

If orientation makes distress worse, stop talking.

5. Offer a two-option choice only if choice is possible

“Space or quiet company?”

“Door open or closed?”

“Text or no words?”

If the person cannot choose, reduce the demand further.

6. Do not touch without clear permission

When sensory overload and trauma may both be present, surprise touch has little upside.

7. Watch what helps

If less input helps, continue reducing input.

If calm orientation helps, continue gently.

If presence helps but words do not, stay quietly.

If presence increases fear or overload, step back while preserving safety.

8. Make no final interpretation during the episode

Do not announce, “This is a meltdown, not trauma,” or “You're having a flashback.” A label can become another argument.

Use neutral language:

- “Something is too much.”
- “We don't have to name it right now.”
- “I am reducing pressure.”
- “We can work out what happened later.”

9. Review the pattern later

After recovery, ask together:

- What happened in the hour before?
- Was there a trauma reminder?
- What sensory or social load was already present?
- What happened to speech?
- What response helped first?

- What made things worse?
- What should we change in the written plan?

Mixed/Unclear Protocol: Pocket Version

Safety. Pause content. Reduce words and sensory load. Give one gentle present-time cue. Offer space or quiet company. No surprise touch. Observe. Name it later.

The Five Assets on One Page

The Moment Map

Safety → What built up? → Where is capacity moving? → What lowers distress?

Meltdown

Subtract input. Fewer words. No debate. No uninvited touch. Recovery first. Accountability later.

Shutdown

Stop demanding speech. Lower bandwidth. Give space. Use a return signal. Resume the issue when capacity returns.

Flashback

Stop the conflict. Orient gently to the present. Offer personalised grounding. Do not interrogate memory. Keep touch consensual.

Mixed/Unclear

Use the lowest-risk common response: safety, less sensory load, fewer words, one present-time cue, and a choice between space and quiet company.

The rest of this book teaches you how to recognise the context around these tools, personalise them, repair what happens around them, and keep your own life intact.

Introduction: When You Don't Know What This Moment Needs

Marlowe Quinn was standing three steps from the kitchen door when the conversation stopped making sense.

A few minutes earlier, the disagreement had been ordinary. The dishwasher had not been emptied. Marlowe had asked about it. Her partner, Sloane Everly, had said he would do it later. Marlowe had answered, more sharply than she intended, that "later" had become the answer to everything that week.

Then Sloane changed.

He stopped looking toward her. His hands moved to his ears. His breathing became quick. When Marlowe asked whether he was listening, he said nothing. When she asked whether he wanted her to leave, he said nothing again. His face had the flat, far-away look Marlowe had learned to fear.

Her mind produced five explanations in less than a minute.

He is shutting down.

He is angry and refusing to talk.

I triggered a trauma memory.

He is about to have a meltdown.

He does not care what this is doing to me.

Each explanation suggested a different response. Give him space. Stay close. Ground him. Keep talking. Stop talking. Ask what he needs. Do not ask anything. Finish the conflict so avoidance does not win. End the conflict because his nervous system is overloaded.

Marlowe felt her own chest tighten. The more uncertain she became, the more she wanted an answer from Sloane. The more she asked, the less he could answer. Within minutes, two nervous systems were trying to solve each other.

Fictional composite case.

If this scene feels familiar, you already understand the reason for this book.

The problem is not that you have failed to read enough about autism. It is not necessarily that you have failed to understand trauma. You may know a great deal about both. The problem is that real relationships do not arrange themselves into separate chapters.

An autistic person can have trauma. A trauma reminder can arrive on a day already overloaded with noise, social demand, pain, masking, and fatigue. A shutdown can occur during an argument whose content still matters. A person in a flashback can also be sensitive to light, touch, tone, and verbal demand. A partner witnessing all this can have their own history of abandonment, criticism, violence, unpredictability, or neurodivergence. Then the neat advice from separate books collides in one room.

That collision is where we begin.

The Question Beneath the Question

Partners often ask, "Was that autism or trauma?"

It is an understandable question. Sometimes the distinction matters. If overload is the main process, reducing sensory and cognitive input may help. If trauma re-experiencing is central, present-time orientation and chosen grounding may help. If the person has shut down, repeated demands for verbal reassurance can worsen the very loss of speech that frightens the other partner.

But the question can also become a trap.

You may never be able to know with certainty what caused a particular moment from the outside. Even clinicians can face difficulty when symptoms overlap or when trauma-related changes are attributed to autism. Research with autistic adults has found high exposure to traumatic events and elevated PTSD symptoms, while research and clinical literature warn that PTSD can be overlooked in autistic people (Andrzejewski et al., 2024; Kildahl & Helverschou, 2024).

A romantic partner cannot solve that problem by becoming more confident in amateur diagnosis.

You need a different question:

> **What response has the best chance of reducing pressure and protecting both of us while we work out what is happening?**

That is the question the Moment Map answers.

State Before Story

Suppose your partner has gone silent during a conflict.

The story your mind tells may be: *They are punishing me.*

Their story may be: *I cannot make language happen.*

Another possibility is: *I am back in the room where my former partner trapped me.*

Or: *The extractor fan, fluorescent light, two hours of social contact, three changes of plan, and this argument have pushed me past capacity.*

Or all of these processes may be partly present.

You cannot settle the story while one or both people have lost enough capacity that discussion itself becomes additional load.

So this book asks you to work in sequence:

6. Establish safety.
7. Respond to current capacity.
8. Allow recovery.
9. Return to meaning, impact, and responsibility later.

The sequence is not an excuse to avoid hard conversations. It is the way you make hard conversations more possible.

Love Is Not the Same as Regulation

There is another reason this book begins with a response system rather than with a long explanation of diagnostic categories.

Partners can slowly become full-time regulators without noticing it.

You learn the tone that prevents an explosion. You cancel plans before your partner becomes overwhelmed. You explain social situations in advance. You handle the phone calls. You stop bringing up certain subjects at night, then in the morning, then on workdays, then on weekends. You watch facial expressions. You scan for changes in breathing. You carry headphones, food, medication, backup plans, explanations, excuses, and guilt.

Some of these accommodations may be loving and sensible. Relationships always involve adaptation. Neurodivergent relationships may require more explicit adaptation because the assumptions one partner makes automatically may not work for the other.

But adaptation can quietly become overfunctioning.

PTSD family research describes "partner accommodation": loved ones may change their own behaviour to reduce distress or help the person avoid trauma reminders. It is usually well-intended, but in some circumstances it can contribute to avoidance and place growing burden on the partner (VA, n.d.-c). The same broad relational danger exists when all autistic needs are managed by one spouse while the autistic adult has no role in planning, communicating, repairing, or seeking support.

This book will not ask you to become better at disappearing.

Two Truths at Once

You will encounter the following pair of truths repeatedly:

> **Dysregulation is not a moral failure.**
>
> **Dysregulation does not make another person's suffering irrelevant.**

A meltdown is not a tantrum performed to control you. A shutdown is not automatically calculated stonewalling. A flashback is not a choice to live in the past.

And yet:

Being screamed at can hurt.

Being frightened by broken objects can change how safe a home feels.

Being unable to discuss finances, parenting, sex, chores, fidelity, substance use, or boundaries because every difficult subject ends in dysregulation can damage a relationship.

Both truths must remain on the page.

Books that keep only the first truth can teach a partner to tolerate too much.

Books that keep only the second can pathologise autistic or traumatised people as difficult, manipulative, cold, or dangerous.

Our task is harder and more useful: understand state accurately enough to respond with care, then return to adult responsibility when enough capacity is available.

Why Autism and Trauma Are Easy to Confuse

Autism is a lifelong neurodevelopmental condition. Trauma-related disorders are not forms of autism. They develop in relation to traumatic exposure and involve patterns such as re-experiencing, avoidance, and ongoing threat. In ICD-11, CPTSD includes the PTSD pattern plus additional disturbances involving emotion regulation, self-concept, and relationships (WHO, 2024a).

The conditions are different.

Their outward signs, however, can overlap.

An autistic person may avoid a place because it is painfully noisy. A person with PTSD may avoid it because it resembles where an assault occurred. An autistic person may become hyper-alert in a chaotic sensory environment. A traumatised person may become hyper-alert because the environment contains a threat reminder. Someone may withdraw because speech has become inaccessible under overload. Someone else may withdraw because closeness feels dangerous. The same person may do all of these things at different times.

The difference often becomes clearer through history, context, timing, and what helps—not through one visible behaviour.

That is why Chapter 1 begins with two histories rather than one label.

What This Book Will Ask of Your Partner

Although you are the primary reader, this is not a book in which one adult studies the other adult like a difficult machine.

The strongest version of every protocol is collaborative.

Your partner has work too:

- identifying early warning signs where possible;
- communicating preferred responses when calm;
- accepting reasonable safety limits;
- returning to important discussions after shutdown or overload;

- participating in repair after harmful episodes;
- seeking appropriate professional treatment for trauma when needed;
- helping build a home that works for both nervous systems.

You cannot complete those tasks on another adult's behalf.

If your partner refuses every form of planning, accountability, treatment, communication, and repair while expecting you to absorb the consequences, the problem is no longer simply that you need a better meltdown protocol.

What This Book Will Ask of You

Your work is different.

You will learn to notice before interpreting.

You will reduce verbal demand when language is failing rather than increasing demand because you are frightened.

You will stop trying to win an argument from inside a nervous-system emergency.

You will examine your own patterns of pursuit, withdrawal, appeasement, rescue, control, and self-erasure.

You will learn the difference between giving time and accepting indefinite avoidance.

You will make safety rules that do not disappear when someone is distressed.

You will build a life in which love has room for two people.

A Better Measure of Progress

Do not judge success by whether dysregulation disappears completely.

That standard can produce shame and concealment. It can also make normal autistic needs look like treatment failures.

A more useful set of questions is:

- Are we noticing overload earlier?
- Are episodes less dangerous?
- Are we adding less pressure during them?
- Are we recovering more effectively?

- Are we returning to important subjects instead of abandoning them?
- Are apologies becoming more specific?
- Are prevention plans changing after new information?
- Is the supporting partner less hypervigilant?
- Is the autistic trauma survivor carrying more of their own adult responsibility?
- Does the relationship contain pleasure, rest, friendship, sex or affection where desired, shared decisions, and separate lives—not only symptom management?

These are relationship outcomes. They matter.

Your First Action

Before Chapter 1, choose three episodes from the last year that left you confused.

For each, write only observable facts:

Before: What happened in the hours before?

During: What changed in movement, speech, attention, breathing, volume, contact, or orientation?

After: What seemed to help? What made things worse? How long did recovery take?

Do not write “He was manipulative,” “She was triggered,” or “They had a shutdown” yet.

Write what a camera and microphone could have recorded.

You are beginning the skill that runs through the whole book: observation before interpretation.

The dishwasher can wait.

So can the argument.

First, learn to read the moment.

Before You Use the Framework on Someone Else

There is one final preparation step. Use the Moment Map on yourself.

Think about the last conflict in which you became highly activated. What was building before you spoke sharply, followed your partner, shut a door, sent ten messages, or gave up? Where did your own capacity move? Did you become louder and more urgent? Did you go quiet and disappear? Did an older fear enter the room? What reduced your pressure?

This exercise matters because no partner is a neutral observer. Your history, sensory profile, attachment patterns, neurodivergence, fatigue, and fear all affect what you see. If you believe silence always means rejection, you will experience shutdown through that lens. If loud voices remind you of earlier danger, a partner's meltdown may activate your own threat system before you can remember a protocol.

The book will ask you to be observant, not detached. You are in the relationship too.

A useful private sentence is: **"I may be reading this accurately, and I may also be activated."**

That sentence creates enough humility to choose safety before certainty.

Part I: Understanding the Two Systems

Chapter 1: One Person, Two Histories

Why can a person be autistic from childhood and still become recognisably different after trauma?

The answer matters because partners often fall into one of two errors. They interpret every difficult reaction through autism, or they interpret every difficult reaction through trauma. Both flatten a more complicated life.

Autism and trauma do not occupy separate bodies. They meet in one person with one sensory system, one history, one set of relationships, and one current environment. To support that person well, you need to know what belongs to long-standing neurodevelopmental difference, what appears to have changed after trauma, and where the two interact.

Autism Is Not a Trauma Response

Autism is a neurodevelopmental condition. Its features begin in the developmental period, even when they are not recognised until adulthood. An adult may receive a diagnosis at thirty-five or fifty-five without having "become autistic" at that age. Late diagnosis often means that earlier traits were masked, misunderstood, compensated for, or interpreted through other explanations.

This matters in relationships because a late diagnosis can make everything look newly medical.

Perhaps your partner has always needed long recovery after social events. Perhaps they have always disliked fluorescent lighting, unexpected visitors, phone calls, certain fabrics, overlapping conversations, or plans that change without warning. Perhaps they have always communicated more clearly in writing than in a fast emotional exchange. A diagnosis may give those patterns a name. It did not create them.

Trauma can then alter the same person's threshold, expectations, and sense of danger.

Trauma Is Not Simply "Bad Stress"

People use the word trauma broadly in everyday speech. Clinically, trauma-related disorders involve specific patterns after exposure to events experienced as threatening or horrific. PTSD includes re-experiencing the traumatic event, avoidance, and a persistent sense of threat. ICD-11 CPTSD includes the PTSD features plus enduring problems in emotion regulation, negative self-concept, and relationships (WHO, 2024a).

A partner does not need to memorise criteria. You do need to understand the basic distinction between a lifelong processing style and an acquired threat pattern.

Consider two versions of the same behaviour.

Elowen Blake avoids a busy railway station because the announcements echo, the lights flicker, people brush against her, and the shifting platform information demands rapid switching. She has disliked stations since childhood.

After being assaulted on a platform, the same station also carries a trauma reminder. Now the sound of a particular announcement produces terror, intrusive sensory fragments, and an urgent need to escape.

The environment did not stop being sensory. The trauma did not erase autism. The station now activates both histories.

Fictional composite case.

The Lifelong Pattern and the Changed Pattern

One of the simplest tools for couples after late diagnosis is a two-column history.

In the first column, write **Lifelong or long-standing**.

In the second, write **Changed after trauma, burnout, illness, or major stress.**

Examples in the first column may include:

- longstanding sensory sensitivities;
- preference for routine;
- intense or highly focused interests;

- direct communication style;
- need for recovery after social interaction;
- difficulty switching attention quickly;
- repetitive movement used for regulation;
- literal interpretation in some contexts;
- longstanding food, clothing, sound, or touch preferences.

Examples in the second may include:

- nightmares beginning after a particular event;
- avoidance of reminders that were previously tolerated;
- sudden fear of a particular type of person, room, smell, or argument;
- new startle responses;
- re-experiencing;
- increased shame or negative beliefs linked to the trauma;
- loss of function during a period of burnout;
- a major reduction in tolerance after prolonged stress.

The purpose is not to make the columns perfectly clean. It is to stop treating the present as if it had no timeline.

When Symptoms Borrow Each Other's Clothing

A difficulty in this field is that one process can resemble another.

Withdrawal is a good example.

Autistic withdrawal may be a response to social and sensory saturation. Trauma-related avoidance may be organised around a threat reminder. Depression can also produce withdrawal. A shutdown may reduce speech. Dissociation can reduce responsiveness. A person may choose ordinary solitude because they enjoy it.

The behaviour "stayed in bedroom for four hours" does not tell you the mechanism.

The same is true of hyperarousal.

Autistic sensory overload can produce intense physiological distress. PTSD can involve persistent threat sensitivity and hyperarousal. Anxiety can heighten both. Sleep deprivation can lower tolerance. Pain can make every demand harder.

Researchers studying autism and trauma have warned that trauma-related symptoms may be misattributed to autism, a problem often described as diagnostic overshadowing (Kildahl & Helverschou, 2024). A 2024 study also found that autistic adults in its sample reported more traumatic events and higher PTSD symptoms than non-autistic adults, reinforcing the need to take trauma assessment seriously rather than assuming that distress is "just autism" (Andrzejewski et al., 2024).

For a partner, the practical lesson is modest: **notice change**.

If a familiar autistic trait changes sharply after an event, do not automatically normalise it as autism. If a behaviour has been present since early life, do not automatically turn it into evidence of trauma.

The Cost of One-Frame Thinking

When autism is the only frame, a partner may say:

"That's just how their brain works."

Sometimes that sentence reduces blame. Sometimes it prevents needed treatment.

When trauma is the only frame, a partner may say:

"If we heal the trauma, all of this will go away."

That can become a demand for the autistic person to become more neurotypical as proof of recovery.

Neither is fair.

Trauma treatment should not aim to remove autistic sensory needs, communication style, focused interests, or legitimate need for recovery. Autism support should not treat nightmares, re-experiencing, trauma avoidance, or post-traumatic fear as fixed autistic traits that cannot change.

The person deserves both forms of understanding.

Two Systems, One Threshold

Think of capacity as a changing threshold rather than a fixed personality trait.

An autistic person may have a high need for predictability. On a rested day, an unexpected change is irritating but manageable. During burnout, the same change may push the system into shutdown.

A person with CPTSD may tolerate conflict reasonably well when rested and secure. After a week of poor sleep and a trauma anniversary, the same tone of voice may activate intense threat.

Now combine the two.

Sensory overload increases arousal. Trauma-related hyperarousal increases sensitivity to the environment. Poor sleep reduces tolerance. Masking consumes energy. A conflict adds social and cognitive demand. A reminder of past threat changes the meaning of the conflict.

The final visible reaction may have several causes.

That is not an argument for giving up on understanding. It is an argument for abandoning simplistic causation.

The Problem With Asking "Which One Is It?" Too Early

During an episode, partners often want a label because labels reduce their own uncertainty.

"Is this a meltdown?"

"Are you triggered?"

"Are you dissociating?"

"Is this a shutdown?"

Those questions may be impossible to answer while the person is dysregulated. They can also feel invasive or accusatory.

The Moment Map asks for something easier: what was building, where capacity is moving, and what reduces pressure.

You can investigate meaning later.

A Note on Dissociation

Dissociation deserves care because it is often used loosely online. Experiences of detachment, unreality, altered awareness, or memory disruption can occur in trauma-related conditions, but they can also occur in other clinical contexts. A partner should not diagnose dissociation from quietness, staring, or reduced speech alone.

If episodes involve significant memory gaps, loss of awareness, severe disorientation, or other concerning changes, professional assessment matters. The same is true for new episodes that could have a neurological, medication-related, substance-related, or medical explanation.

This book deliberately keeps the Moment Map broad enough that you do not need to settle that question in the living room.

When the Relationship Becomes Part of the Threat System

Trauma is relational for many people. Threat may have occurred in childhood attachment relationships, previous partnerships, institutions, families, or communities. As a result, ordinary intimacy can contain reminders: dependence, disagreement, sex, money, doors closing, someone raising their voice, someone going quiet, being watched, being corrected, being asked where you have been.

The current partner may become associated with old threat even when they are not behaving abusively.

But there is a boundary here that must remain visible.

If the current relationship is actually frightening, controlling, violent, or coercive, do not explain present danger as merely a trauma memory. A trauma history can make threat systems sensitive, but sometimes the threat is current.

Safety assessment always comes before interpretation.

The Two-History Exercise

Take a sheet of paper and draw a vertical line.

On the left, write **Long-standing autistic pattern**.

On the right, write **Trauma-linked or later change**.

Then add a third section beneath both: **Interaction**.

In the interaction section, write examples where both may matter.

For example:

Long-standing: sensitive to shouting.

Later change: panic after a violent previous relationship.

Interaction: raised voices now create both sensory pain and trauma threat.

Or:

Long-standing: needs preparation for changes.

Later change: betrayal trauma increased fear of uncertainty.

Interaction: an unexplained late return home is both an unexpected schedule change and a threat cue.

The third section is often where the relationship actually lives.

What to Carry Forward

You are not loving two separate people: an autistic person and a trauma survivor.

You are loving one person whose nervous system has a developmental history and a lived history.

That person may need lower sensory load and trauma treatment. They may need routine and the freedom to change old threat beliefs. They may need communication accommodations and accountability. They may need solitude and secure attachment.

The Moment Map works because it does not force those needs into competition.

It asks what is happening now, while the chapters ahead teach you how the past shaped what "now" can hold.

A Third History: The Relationship Itself

There is another timeline to add beside autism and trauma: the history the couple has created together.

Repeated episodes teach both partners what to expect. If one person has often disappeared after conflict, the other may begin every pause already afraid that the conversation will never resume. If one person has repeatedly been pursued during shutdown, they may begin shutting down earlier because the first signs of conflict predict being followed. If a trauma flashback has led to accusations that were never repaired, the supporting partner may become defensive the moment trauma language appears.

These learned expectations are not necessarily autism or CPTSD. They are relationship conditioning.

This matters because couples sometimes search only inside the diagnosed partner for the mechanism. Yet a pattern can become self-maintaining between two people. One partner predicts abandonment and pursues. The other predicts pursuit and withdraws. Each person's protection confirms the other's fear.

The good news is that relationship history can also be rewritten through repeated safer experiences. A return signal used reliably ten times begins to mean something. A partner who actually stops talking when the shutdown card appears becomes more predictable. An autistic partner who returns to the financial discussion the next morning shows that pausing is not avoidance. A trauma survivor who tells the partner, after recovery, "I know you were not the person from my past," repairs the present relationship.

The relationship is not only the place symptoms appear. It can become a place new expectations are learned.

How to Talk About Cause Without Pretending to Know Too Much

Couples often want causal language because it seems to settle blame. "The autism caused it." "The trauma caused it." "My tone caused it." In most real episodes, cause is distributed.

A more accurate vocabulary separates **contributing factors**, **triggering events**, and **maintaining responses**.

A contributing factor may be low sleep or burnout. A triggering event may be an unexpected change or trauma reminder. A maintaining response may be the partner continuing to argue after language has become inaccessible. These are not interchangeable.

Consider a meltdown after a family dinner. The dinner was noisy. The autistic partner had masked all afternoon. A relative made a comment that resembled earlier emotional abuse. The spouse then asked for an explanation in the car while music was playing. Which factor caused the meltdown? The question may have no useful single answer.

Try language such as:

- "The noise seems to have contributed."
- "The comment may have been a trauma reminder."
- "My questions added demand after your speech was already reducing."
- "We do not know how much each factor mattered."

This style of language protects both people from false certainty. It also creates more prevention options. If there are four contributing factors, the couple can change several parts of the system rather than searching for one guilty cause.

Clinical assessment may eventually clarify some patterns. Home life does not need to wait for perfect theory before becoming safer.

Chapter 2: The Diagnosis That Changes the Past Without Rewriting It

Briar Knox had been married for fourteen years before one sentence from an assessor reorganised the marriage.

"Your history is consistent with autism."

Briar was not the person being assessed. Her wife, Carys Monroe, was. Yet Briar felt the words land inside her own biography.

Suddenly, memories changed category.

The wedding reception Carys disappeared from for forty minutes was no longer simply the night she "couldn't be bothered with Briar's family." The blank expression during emotional conversations might not have meant indifference. The rigid holiday plans, the headphones, the recovery days after parties, the hours spent preparing for phone calls—each acquired a possible explanation.

Briar felt relief.

Then she felt furious.

If Carys had not meant to reject her all those years, what was Briar supposed to do with the years she had felt rejected?

Fictional composite case.

Late diagnosis can produce a strange form of time travel. It sends a couple backward through the relationship with new information but no ability to change what happened.

Relief Does Not Cancel Grief

For some adults, an autism diagnosis is deeply relieving. It may replace decades of moral explanations—lazy, rude, cold, dramatic, oversensitive, difficult—with a more accurate developmental account. Qualitative research on late-diagnosed autistic adults, particularly women and people who have camouflaged heavily, describes years of misunderstanding before diagnosis and the costs of masking (Bargiela et al., 2016; Hull et al., 2017).

Partners can experience relief too.

A behaviour that looked like lack of love may make more sense as overload. A need for solitude may stop looking like rejection. Direct communication may stop being read as deliberate harshness. The couple may finally have words for recurring patterns.

But relief can coexist with grief.

You may grieve years spent blaming yourself.

You may grieve the fights that occurred because neither of you understood what was happening.

You may grieve the version of partnership you kept trying to create.

You may feel cheated by clinicians, families, schools, or social expectations that missed the diagnosis.

You may also resent the way diagnosis suddenly asks you to reinterpret behaviour that still hurt.

That resentment does not make you anti-autistic. It means explanation and impact are different questions.

The Three Versions of a Memory

A useful way to revisit the past is to hold three versions of a memory at once.

Version 1: What I believed then

"I thought you left the party because you were embarrassed by me."

Version 2: What I understand now

"I now know the noise, conversations, perfume, and unpredictability had pushed you into overload."

Version 3: What the event did to me

"I still spent forty minutes alone at our wedding reception believing my wife did not want to be beside me."

All three can be true.

The diagnosis changes interpretation. It does not erase lived consequence.

This is why "but I'm autistic" cannot be the final sentence in a repair conversation. It may be the beginning of an accurate explanation. Repair still asks: what did this do to the other person, and what can we build differently now?

Trauma Can Also Be Diagnosed Late

CPTSD or PTSD may also be named years after a relationship begins. That diagnosis can produce its own backward revision.

A partner may realise that apparently disproportionate fear during arguments was connected to earlier abuse. Sexual withdrawal may have involved trauma reminders. Reassurance seeking may have been organised around abandonment fear. Anger may have arrived on the edge of terror.

Again, the diagnosis can humanise what previously looked irrational.

And again, it cannot turn the partner into an infinite container.

When trauma is identified late, couples sometimes make a second mistake: they organise the whole relationship around preventing activation.

No raised concerns.

No unexpected plans.

No sexual boundaries that might feel rejecting.

No disagreement about money.

No request for accountability if shame might be triggered.

That is not recovery. It is a family system becoming smaller around fear.

The Difference Between Compassion and Revisionism

Revisionism says: "Now that we know the reason, the past did not hurt."

Compassion says: "Now that we know more, we can understand the behaviour more accurately and still acknowledge its effect."

This distinction allows both partners to remain real.

Carys may say: “I did not leave the reception because I did not love you. I was close to meltdown and did not know what was happening.”

Briar may answer: “I believe you. I also need you to understand why that memory stayed painful.”

The next question is practical: “If we were doing that event now, what would we change?”

That moves the couple from blame to design.

Masking: The Hidden Cost of Looking Fine

Masking or camouflaging can include consciously or unconsciously suppressing autistic behaviours, rehearsing social responses, copying others, forcing eye contact, or hiding distress to meet expected norms. Research with autistic adults has linked camouflaging with exhaustion and negative wellbeing, and many late-diagnosed adults describe years of performing competence while paying a private cost (Hull et al., 2017; Miller et al., 2021).

In relationships, masking creates a confusing pattern.

The partner may see an apparently capable person succeed at work and then collapse at home.

“Why can you hold it together for everyone else but not for me?” becomes a painful question.

One answer can be that home is where the accumulated load is released. That does not make every form of release acceptable. It does explain why the safe person may see more distress than colleagues do.

Another answer is that the autistic person has used so much capacity on public performance that there is little left for domestic flexibility, conversation, chores, or intimacy.

The relationship may need to reduce the amount of masking required outside the home rather than simply demanding better behaviour inside it.

Trauma and Masking Can Reinforce Each Other

A traumatised autistic person may have more than social reasons to mask.

They may have learned that visible distress was punished.

They may hide pain because expressing needs previously led to ridicule, abandonment, or violence.

They may comply automatically when frightened and collapse later.

They may say “I'm fine” because identifying internal states is difficult, because they fear conflict, or both.

This is another reason not to rely only on words spoken under pressure.

The couple needs calm-time systems for noticing load before speech becomes unreliable.

The Partner's Late-Diagnosis Trap

There is a subtle role partners can fall into after diagnosis: retrospective clinician.

Every past argument is analysed.

Every preference is relabelled.

Every family member is reinterpreted.

The partner begins to explain the autistic person's behaviour to them.

“You're not angry. You're overloaded.”

“You only think you want to leave because you're triggered.”

“You're shutting down.”

This can become intrusive even when it begins with care.

The Moment Map is deliberately built to reduce this tendency. It allows you to respond to observable capacity without claiming authority over another person's inner life.

“You don't have to answer right now” is different from “You're in shutdown.”

“I am going to reduce the noise” is different from “Your autism is making you irrational.”

“We can pause and come back” is different from “This is your trauma talking.”

Respect grows in that difference.

Re-Storying Without Erasure

Try the following exercise together if both people can do it without turning the conversation into prosecution.

Choose one recurring relationship problem from before diagnosis.

Each partner completes three sentences:

> **Then I thought...**
>
> **Now I wonder...**
>
> **What still mattered to me was...**

For example:

Briar:

"Then I thought you went silent because you wanted me to suffer."

"Now I wonder whether you had lost speech under overload."

"What still mattered to me was that no one came back to the conversation for two days."

Carys:

"Then I thought you kept following me because you wanted to control me."

"Now I wonder whether my unexplained silence activated your fear of abandonment."

"What still mattered to me was that I had no quiet place where I could recover."

Now add one design sentence:

> **Next time we will...**

"Use the shutdown card and agree on a return time."

That final sentence is where diagnosis becomes useful.

Do Not Make the Past Neater Than It Was

Some relationships improve greatly after late diagnosis because the couple can finally stop fighting the wrong problem.

Others discover that diagnosis explains only part of what went wrong.

There may also have been contempt, incompatibility, substance misuse, untreated depression, infidelity, financial secrecy, coercion, unequal domestic labour, or ordinary human immaturity.

Autism does not absorb every problem around it.

Neither does CPTSD.

A good integrated model should make the relationship more accurate, not more flattering.

From Explanation to Agreement

The useful question after any new diagnosis is not "Who was right about the past?"

It is:

What do we know now that should change how we live next week?

Maybe social events need an exit plan.

Maybe difficult conversations should happen in writing first.

Maybe trauma treatment needs to be added.

Maybe the partner needs their own therapist.

Maybe the house needs a quiet room.

Maybe childcare needs to be redistributed so recovery time does not depend on one partner doing everything.

Maybe the autistic partner needs to stop promising plans they cannot sustain.

Maybe the non-autistic partner needs to stop reading reduced eye contact as dishonesty.

A diagnosis earns its place in a relationship when it improves design.

It should not become a weapon, an excuse, or a new way to argue about the old years.

The Grief Conversation Nobody Schedules

Late diagnosis can produce grief on both sides that does not fit neatly into symptom management. The autistic partner may grieve the years spent believing they were defective. The other partner may grieve years spent trying to obtain forms of closeness that were never going to arise automatically. Both may grieve decisions made without the information they have now.

Do not force this grief into gratitude. "At least we know now" can be true and still arrive too soon.

A structured grief conversation can help. Each person answers three questions without interruption:

10. **What do I wish we had known earlier?**
11. **What did I lose because we did not know?**
12. **What is still possible now?**

The third question prevents grief from becoming a permanent trial of the past. It also prevents diagnosis from becoming a fantasy that everything will now be easy.

Sometimes the answer to "what is still possible" is modest: fewer misunderstandings, a quieter home, more honest plans, less shame. Those changes can be substantial even when the relationship does not transform into the version either person once imagined.

Late diagnosis is not a reset button. It is new information. What the couple does with that information determines whether it becomes relief, resentment, or a more accurate way of living.

When Only One Partner Wants the New Story

Sometimes diagnosis creates asymmetry. One person reads everything. The other avoids the subject. The diagnosed partner may want every past conflict reinterpreted through autism or trauma. The spouse may feel exhausted by psychological language and want ordinary accountability. Or the reverse: the supporting partner becomes intensely interested in diagnosis while the autistic partner does not want their identity reorganised around it.

Do not force shared meaning before shared practice.

A couple can agree on behaviour without agreeing on a grand explanation.

They can agree:

- no difficult conversations after midnight;
- use the shutdown card if speech disappears;
- no uninvited touch during high distress;
- return to paused issues within twenty-four hours when possible;
- keep exits clear;
- use written agendas for money discussions.

These agreements can improve life even if one person says “autistic overload” and the other says “I just run out of capacity.”

Identity language belongs partly to the person whose identity is being described. If your partner prefers “autistic person,” “person with autism,” “neurodivergent,” or no label in ordinary conversation, respect that preference where possible. Trauma language should also be used carefully. A diagnosis is not permission to narrate someone else's childhood publicly or explain their behaviour to relatives without consent.

The new story becomes useful when it creates better treatment of each other, not when both people can recite the same theory.

Chapter 3: The Moment Map in Real Life

Sloane Everly knew more and became less certain.

Before learning about autism and trauma, she had one explanation for her husband's difficult moments: he was angry.

After months of reading, she had six.

Sensory overload. Meltdown. Shutdown. Flashback. Dissociation. Burnout.

Her knowledge had improved. Her confidence had not.

That was progress.

Fictional composite case.

A reliable response model should make you more skilful without making you falsely certain. The Moment Map is built for that kind of competence.

Why a Map, Not a Test

Tests aim to classify.

Maps aim to orient.

When you are driving in heavy rain, you do not need a theory of weather to choose the next safe turn. You need enough information to avoid the ditch and continue toward a destination.

The Moment Map gives you four destinations and a route-selection process. It does not claim that the border between them is sharp.

The four destinations are:

Meltdown. Shutdown. Flashback/trauma activation. Mixed/unclear.

The route begins with safety because no psychological interpretation matters more than immediate physical risk.

Then you ask what built up, where capacity seems to be moving, and what lowers pressure.

Destination One: Meltdown

A meltdown often has a build-up.

National Autistic Society guidance describes a “rumble stage” in which distress may become visible before full meltdown—for example through pacing, repetitive questioning, rocking, or becoming very still (National Autistic Society, 2020).

The important word is **overwhelm**.

The person is not simply having a strong opinion. Capacity has been exceeded.

Common contextual clues may include:

- prolonged sensory exposure;
- many social demands;
- unexpected change;
- interrupted routine;
- pain or illness;
- hunger or sleep loss;
- sustained masking;
- too many decisions;
- emotional conflict added to existing load;
- loss of access to usual regulating strategies.

Outward signs vary widely. Some people cry. Some shout. Some pace or rock intensely. Some need to escape. Some repeat words. Some hit themselves. Some become physically agitated. Others show less dramatic but still obvious loss of control.

The Moment Map does not define meltdown by loudness. It looks for overload plus loss of flexible capacity.

Destination Two: Shutdown

Shutdown often looks like subtraction.

Speech reduces.

Movement reduces.

Choices become harder.

The person may retreat, become still, stop responding, lie down, cover themselves, stare, or rely on very simple communication.

In a relationship, shutdown is especially easy to misread because it can resemble interpersonal withdrawal.

The partner may think:

They are refusing to answer because they know they are wrong.

Sometimes a person is refusing. Adults do sometimes avoid difficult discussions. But shutdown asks a different question: **Can they currently do what I am asking?**

If the answer appears to be no, pressure is unlikely to produce healthy communication.

This is where the return signal becomes central. You protect the current lack of capacity without allowing the subject to disappear indefinitely.

Destination Three: Flashback or Trauma Activation

Trauma re-experiencing changes the time sense of a moment.

A smell, sound, touch, argument, bodily sensation, or relational pattern may evoke a traumatic event with enough intensity that the body responds to the current situation as threat. Flashbacks can involve vivid sensory re-experiencing, but not every trauma response looks cinematic. Some people experience intense emotional and bodily activation with only partial conscious connection to the original event.

Because popular trauma language is broader than formal diagnostic language, this book uses **flashback/trauma activation** when the response appears organised around past threat. That wording is descriptive, not diagnostic.

Clues may include:

- a clear trauma reminder;
- statements that confuse the current situation with past threat;
- intense fear that does not fit the present level of danger;
- urgent escape from perceived entrapment;
- sudden re-experiencing sensations or images;
- fear of touch linked to past harm;
- a pronounced change after a trauma-linked cue.

Again, no single clue proves the category.

Destination Four: Mixed or Unclear

The fourth destination is not a failure to decide. It is the most honest category when the evidence is messy.

Consider this sequence:

An autistic adult has worked an eight-hour customer-facing shift while masking heavily. The train home is delayed and crowded. At home, their partner says, "We need to talk about your spending." The tone resembles a controlling parent from childhood. The autistic partner feels trapped, the refrigerator compressor is whining, the room is too bright, and the conversation requires rapid explanation of several purchases.

What is happening?

Sensory overload is real.

Cognitive demand is real.

Trauma threat is real.

Relationship content is real.

If you insist on selecting one cause, you lose useful information.

The mixed protocol says: lower load, orient gently, stop the conflict, keep exits open, avoid touch, and name the pattern later.

The Four Questions in Practice

Let us walk through three examples.

Example A: The Restaurant

Arden Blythe and Pippa Sterling are at a restaurant. It is louder than expected. A birthday group is shouting. The waiter has changed their table. Pippa's meal arrives with a sauce she cannot tolerate. She begins rocking faster, presses her hands over her ears, repeats "no, no, no," and cannot answer whether she wants a replacement meal.

Safety: No immediate physical danger.

What built up: Strong sensory load, unexpected change, food problem.

Where capacity is moving: Outward distress, language and decision-making reducing.

What lowers pressure: Leaving the restaurant, fewer words, quiet car.

A meltdown formulation is plausible. The useful response is not to ground Pippa through a trauma narrative. It is to get out of the overloaded environment.

Example B: The Bedroom Door

Wren Hollis and Tamsin Hayes are arguing. Tamsin closes the bedroom door to keep the dog out. Wren's expression changes instantly. She backs into the wall and says, "Open it. Open it. Don't lock me in." Tamsin has not locked the door. Wren is breathing rapidly and does not seem able to take in reassurance about the argument.

Safety: Open the door. Increase distance.

What built up: Conflict plus a specific entrapment cue.

Where capacity is moving: Past threat appears to be entering the present.

What lowers pressure: Open exit, factual orientation, no touch.

Trauma activation is plausible.

Example C: The Silence

Marlowe Quinn asks Briar Knox whether they can discuss a credit-card bill. Briar has had three nights of poor sleep and a difficult week at work. She looks at the bill, stops speaking, lies down on the sofa, and covers her face. When Marlowe asks if she is angry, Briar makes a small gesture meaning "stop." Ninety minutes later she texts, "Words gone. Not leaving. Tomorrow 10?"

Safety: Intact.

What built up: fatigue, work stress, cognitively demanding conversation.

Where capacity is moving: inward, with speech loss.

What lowers pressure: no questions, rest, written return signal.

Shutdown is plausible.

None of these examples is a diagnosis. Each is a response decision.

Watch the Preceding Hour, Not Only the Preceding Sentence

Couples often identify the "trigger" as the last thing said.

That can be misleading.

The last sentence may have been one gram placed on a scale already holding a kilogram.

Autistic burnout research is useful here because it describes cumulative load rather than one dramatic cause. Raymaker and colleagues' participants described burnout in terms of chronic exhaustion, lost skills, reduced tolerance to stimulus, and expectations that outstripped available resources (Raymaker et al., 2020).

Even outside full burnout, cumulative load matters.

Ask:

What was sleep like?

How much social contact occurred?

Was there pain?

Were plans changed?

How much masking was required?

Was there a trauma anniversary?

Did the person eat?

Were there several unresolved conflicts already active?

The preceding hour can be too short. Sometimes you need the preceding week.

Watch Function, Not Appearance

Two people can look completely different during meltdown.

Two shutdowns can look different.

Two flashbacks can look different.

Your map should therefore become personalised.

Do not write “meltdown = shouting” if your partner's overload usually appears as frantic cleaning and repeated speech.

Do not write “shutdown = lying down” if your partner keeps moving but loses language.

Do not write “flashback = crying” if your partner becomes cold, defensive, and urgently controlling of exits when frightened.

The correct map is built from repeated observations and your partner's own account when calm.

Use Response as a Clue, Not a Test

If noise reduction helps quickly, that supports the idea that sensory load matters.

If an open door and present-time cue help, trauma threat may be central.

If text becomes possible before speech, shutdown may be involved.

But do not deliberately provoke or withhold support to “test” your theory.

The purpose of observing response is to learn naturally from what you are already doing.

The Danger of Label Fighting

In some couples, the label becomes a new argument.

“You were having a meltdown.”

“No, I wasn't.”

“You were triggered.”

“Stop psychoanalysing me.”

The Moment Map does not require agreement on a label during the event.

Try neutral language:

“Something became too much.”

"Words look hard right now."

"I am going to stop the discussion."

"I am opening the door and moving back."

"We can name what happened later."

Neutral language keeps the protocol from becoming a diagnosis imposed by the partner.

The Red Flag That Overrides the Map

There is one category that does not sit on the map because it changes the task entirely: **current abuse or coercive control**.

If someone uses threats, intimidation, stalking, financial control, sexual coercion, physical violence, deliberate property destruction, blocking of exits, or fear to control the other person, do not spend your energy deciding whether the behaviour is "really" meltdown or trauma.

A person can be autistic, traumatised, and abusive.

A person can also have a frightening-looking meltdown without engaging in a pattern of coercive control.

The distinction matters, and Chapter 9 addresses it directly.

For now, remember: if you are unsafe, safety outranks classification.

Build Your Personal Map

Return to the three episodes you recorded after the Introduction.

For each, answer:

Safety

What risk was present? What did each person need physically?

Build-up

List sensory, social, cognitive, physical, emotional, and trauma-related load in the previous day.

Capacity direction

Did speech increase, repeat, reduce, or disappear?

Did movement expand or contract?

Did the person seem oriented to the current place and relationship?

Helpful response

What reduced distress?

Unhelpful response

What increased pressure?

Later account

What did your partner say happened internally, if they could describe it?

Plan change

What will you do differently next time?

Do not worry if one episode remains mixed.

The map is working when it helps you choose a better next move, not when it gives every event a tidy label.

Common Moment-Map Errors

A framework becomes useful when you know how it can be misused. Watch for five errors.

Error 1: Choosing the label from one behaviour

Silence does not equal shutdown. Shouting does not equal meltdown. Fear does not equal flashback. Always look at context, change in capacity, and what came before.

Error 2: Ignoring the partner's own account

Your observation matters, but the person who experienced the episode has information you do not. If they later say, "I could hear you; I just could not make words," that should update your map. If they say, "I was not in a flashback; I was angry that you blocked the door," take that seriously too.

Error 3: Using the map to win arguments

"You are dysregulated, therefore I am right" is not a valid conclusion. Capacity and content are separate questions. A person can be overloaded and correct about the underlying issue.

Error 4: Treating the map as permanent

Signs change with age, burnout, therapy, medication, environment, and life circumstances. Review the map rather than preserving an outdated profile.

Error 5: Forgetting ordinary explanations

Sometimes a person is tired. Sometimes they are angry. Sometimes they do not want to talk. Sometimes they forgot. Not every difficult moment belongs on a clinical map.

The framework should make the relationship less pathologised, not more.

The Three-Column Observation Log

For four weeks, if episodes are frequent enough to justify tracking, use three columns rather than a diary full of interpretations.

Column 1: Before

Record facts: sleep, workday, social activity, sensory environment, meals, pain, conflict, trauma reminders, medication changes, alcohol or other substances if relevant.

Column 2: During

Record observable changes: speech shortened, pacing began, eye contact reduced, person moved toward exit, repeated phrase, crying, hands over ears, confusion about current situation, silence, hiding, rapid breathing.

Column 3: What helped

Record what actually reduced demand or increased orientation: lights off, partner left room, door opened, text instead of speech, headphones, present-time cue, sleep, food, no touch.

Do not turn the log into evidence for prosecution. The purpose is pattern recognition. If the autistic partner is willing, compare it with their internal account later. You may discover that an outward sign means something different than you assumed.

You may also discover that your own behaviour appears in the pattern. Perhaps repeated reassurance questions consistently precede deeper shutdown. Perhaps leaving without a return signal intensifies trauma panic. Perhaps certain discussions occur only when both people are tired.

Data in a relationship should create curiosity, not surveillance. Stop tracking if it becomes obsessive, punitive, or a substitute for living.

Part II: What to Do in the Moment

Chapter 4: Catching the Rumble Before the Crash

Three objects sat on Pippa Sterling's kitchen counter: a set of noise-cancelling headphones, an unopened protein bar, and a folded card that said **NO WORDS - SAFE - NEED 30 MINUTES**.

None of them looked like relationship tools.

Together, they had prevented more arguments than any communication exercise Pippa and her partner had tried.

Fictional composite case.

Most couples begin learning about dysregulation at the peak. The voice is already raised. Speech is already gone. Someone is crying, pacing, hiding, shaking, or leaving. At that point the available choices are narrower.

Prevention begins earlier, when the problem is still a rising load rather than a full loss of capacity.

The Rumble Stage Is Personal

Autism guidance sometimes uses the term "rumble stage" for early signs of distress before a meltdown. The National Autistic Society notes that people may show changes such as pacing, repetitive questioning, rocking, or becoming very still before the peak (National Autistic Society, 2020).

The phrase is useful as long as you do not expect everyone to rumble in the same way.

One person becomes louder.

Another becomes unusually agreeable.

One paces.

Another freezes.

One starts repeating a complaint.

Another begins making mistakes in routine tasks.

One asks for reassurance.

Another becomes intensely literal and unable to tolerate ambiguity.

The earliest sign may be something only the autistic person can feel: pressure behind the eyes, heat, buzzing skin, slowed language, nausea, a need to flee, or the sense that every sound has become sharp.

Your goal is not to monitor your partner like a weather station. It is to build shared recognition.

The Load Is Often Cumulative

Couples frequently argue about the final demand because that is the event both can see.

"Why did asking you to put your shoes away cause a meltdown?"

It may not have.

Perhaps the day contained:

- poor sleep;
- a scratchy shirt worn for work;
- an unexpected meeting;
- fluorescent lighting;
- lunch skipped because the cafeteria was crowded;
- three phone calls;
- a delayed train;
- an unfamiliar route home;
- a neighbour's drilling;
- an unresolved text from a parent;
- an upcoming trauma anniversary;
- no time alone since waking.

Then came the shoes.

The shoes are easy to blame because the shoes arrived last.

A better model is a **load stack**.

Each demand takes some capacity. Some demands also prevent recovery. When the remaining margin becomes thin, a small event can produce a large response without being the main cause.

Autistic burnout research makes this cumulative logic especially visible. Raymaker and colleagues described burnout as arising when life stressors and barriers to relief create a mismatch between expectations and available abilities (Raymaker et al., 2020). You do not need to be in full burnout for the same principle to matter on a smaller scale.

Six Kinds of Load

Use six categories when reviewing a difficult day.

1. Sensory load

Noise, lighting, touch, smells, temperature, clothing, crowds, visual clutter, traffic, alarms, appliances, children yelling, or overlapping speech.

2. Social load

Meetings, customer service, family gatherings, hosting, small talk, interpreting indirect communication, being watched, performing expected facial expressions, or prolonged interaction without recovery.

3. Cognitive load

Decision-making, switching tasks, paperwork, planning, navigating unfamiliar places, remembering multiple instructions, rapid verbal discussion, or solving several problems at once.

4. Physical load

Sleep loss, illness, hormonal changes, pain, hunger, dehydration, medication changes, substance use, or physical exertion.

5. Emotional load

Conflict, grief, shame, uncertainty, financial worry, parenting stress, work pressure, rejection, disappointment, or anticipation of a difficult event.

6. Trauma load

Reminders, anniversaries, contact with unsafe people, therapy sessions, legal processes, family visits, news events, bodily sensations, sexual situations, or conflict patterns linked to past danger.

The categories overlap. That is fine. Their purpose is to widen your attention.

The Load Audit Must Not Become Surveillance

There is a relational danger in learning early signs: the supporting partner becomes the manager.

"You've had enough socialising."

"You're getting overloaded."

"You need to eat."

"You're doing the thing you do before a meltdown."

Even accurate observations can feel controlling when one adult constantly assesses another.

The better arrangement is shared ownership.

The autistic partner might use a number, colour, or phrase:

Green: normal flexibility.

Amber: capacity narrowing; reduce optional demand.

Red: no conflict discussion; recovery only.

Or:

Bandwidth 8/10: plenty available.

Bandwidth 4/10: keep plans simple.

Bandwidth 1/10: essential communication only.

The supporting partner can report their own bandwidth too.

That matters. If one partner is at 2/10 and the other is at 3/10, neither should be assigned the job of regulating both people.

Trauma Warning Signs Can Be Different

Early trauma activation may show up as scanning, startle, sudden suspicion, urgency, bodily tension, a need to control exits, rapid reassurance seeking, emotional numbing, or abrupt withdrawal.

A reminder may not be conscious at first.

This is where partners can make a costly mistake: they respond to the literal content without noticing the state change.

Suppose Carys Monroe says, “Why are you standing there like that?”

Her partner says, “Like what?”

Carys becomes more agitated. “Don't do that. Don't stand between me and the door.”

The literal dispute could become, “I'm not blocking the door. You're being ridiculous.”

The state-based response is different: move away from the door first. Discuss perception later.

The Supporting Partner Has a Rumble Stage Too

This may be the most neglected part of prevention.

What happens in your body before you pursue, criticise, rescue, lecture, appease, or shut down?

Maybe your early signs are:

- talking faster;
- repeating the same question;
- following your partner from room to room;
- demanding reassurance;
- explaining too much;
- becoming sarcastic;
- feeling heat in your face;
- mentally rehearsing every past incident;
- taking over tasks angrily;
- saying “fine” when you are not fine;
- becoming desperate to resolve the issue before sleep.

Your nervous system also shapes the episode.

A shutdown can activate your abandonment fear. A raised voice can activate your own trauma. A blank expression can feel like contempt. Repetition can make you feel trapped. When both people reach the red zone, even a good protocol can become hard to use.

Your personal warning sign may need its own card:

When I start asking the same question three times, I need to stop the conversation.

That is not surrender. It is skill.

The Difference Between Prevention and Avoidance

If the couple discovers that financial conversations frequently overload one partner, what should they do?

Avoid money forever?

No.

Change the conditions.

Maybe discuss one account at a time.

Send numbers in writing before the meeting.

Choose a quiet time.

Set a twenty-minute limit.

Remove background noise.

Allow written responses.

Do not combine the money discussion with criticism about chores, sex, and in-laws.

Prevention changes the route to necessary conversations. Avoidance removes necessary conversations from the relationship.

The distinction is important in trauma too. PTSD treatment often works in part by reducing patterns of trauma-related avoidance through evidence-based approaches delivered by clinicians (VA, n.d.-b). A partner should not become an exposure therapist, but neither should the household become organised around never encountering any discomfort.

Create a "Not Today" Rule

Some days are bad days for high-stakes conversations.

A "not today" rule can be helpful if it includes a return plan.

Not today because: sleep was two hours, work was chaotic, and speech is already slowing.

Return: Saturday at 11 a.m., by text first, twenty minutes maximum.

This differs from indefinite postponement.

A pause without a return point breeds mistrust. A pause with a reliable return point protects capacity.

Early Intervention Is Often Ordinary

Prevention rarely looks dramatic.

It may be:

- eating before the difficult appointment;
- declining a second social event;
- wearing headphones in the supermarket;
- using the same parking place;
- taking thirty minutes alone after work;
- writing the agenda before a relationship meeting;
- sleeping separately after a trauma-triggering nightmare;
- changing the lightbulb;
- moving an argument out of the car;
- letting a text stand unanswered for an hour;
- rescheduling sex without treating the change as rejection;
- leaving a family gathering at the agreed time.

These choices are small. Their effect can be large because they preserve margin.

The Load and Warning-Sign Map

Create four headings together.

My common load

What reliably uses capacity?

My early signs

What can I notice in myself before I lose flexibility?

Your observable clues

What may my partner notice without telling me what I feel?

Helpful early actions

What should we reduce, stop, add, or postpone?

Keep the language behavioural.

Better: “Speech gets shorter and I start rubbing my hands.”

Worse: “I become impossible.”

Better: “I ask the same reassurance question several times.”

Worse: “I get crazy.”

The purpose is to make early signs usable, not shameful.

When Prevention Fails

You can do everything sensibly and still have a meltdown, shutdown, or flashback.

That does not prove the plan was useless.

Human nervous systems are not machines. Trauma reminders can be unexpected. Illness changes capacity. Life contains emergencies. Children wake at night. Trains are cancelled. People make mistakes.

The goal of prevention is not perfect control.

It is more margin, earlier recognition, and fewer avoidable collisions.

Sometimes the protein bar is not enough.

That is when the next protocol matters.

Prevention in Public, Work, and Travel

Home is only one part of the load system. Many meltdowns and shutdowns occur after the person has already spent hours adapting elsewhere. Prevention therefore sometimes requires changes beyond the relationship.

At work, useful adjustments may include predictable schedules, quieter workspaces, written instructions, reduced hot-desking, planned breaks, or clearer expectations. The exact options depend on the job, disability law in the relevant country, and the person's needs. The partner should not become the employee's unofficial case manager, but it can help to recognise that repeated evening collapse may be telling you something about the workday rather than the marriage.

Travel needs its own load plan. Airports combine noise, uncertainty, queues, security demands, time pressure, crowds, and rapid changes. Build recovery time into the itinerary. Do not schedule the most emotionally demanding family visit immediately after a long journey if that can be avoided. Carry familiar sensory supports in hand luggage rather than checked baggage. Decide in advance what happens if a plan changes.

Public events need exits. A useful agreement is not "we must stay until the end." It is "we will know how either of us can leave without turning departure into a relationship crisis." Two sets of keys, separate transport, or an agreed taxi budget can transform a trapped feeling into choice.

Prevention is often logistical. That is not less meaningful than emotional work. Sometimes the most loving sentence is not "tell me how you feel." It is "we have our own way home."

Recovery Debt

A person can appear recovered enough to function while still carrying a deficit from earlier load. Think of this as **recovery debt**: not a formal clinical diagnosis, but a practical description of capacity that has not fully replenished.

Monday contains a difficult meeting and late train. Tuesday begins with too little sleep. Wednesday brings a family visit. By Thursday, nothing dramatic has happened that day, yet the system has had no real recovery window. The partner may be surprised when an ordinary request produces a shutdown.

This pattern matters especially around burnout. If every available quiet period is filled with chores, appointments, social obligations, or relationship processing, the person may never return to baseline.

Recovery debt also applies to the supporting partner. After several frightening episodes, you may remain on alert even during calm days. Your threshold for another raised voice may be lower. Your patience may be thinner. You may need your own recovery rather than another discussion about how to help your partner better.

A weekly plan should therefore contain deliberate low-demand space for both people, not only crisis recovery after something goes wrong. Rest is easier to protect when it is planned before anyone is desperate for it.

Chapter 5: When Overload Moves Outward

"Stop asking me questions."

"I am asking one question."

"It is still a question."

Tamsin Hayes took a step toward the hallway. Her partner, Romilly Chase, pressed both hands against her temples and began pacing faster.

"Do you want me to leave?" Tamsin asked.

Romilly made a sound that was not quite a word.

"Should I turn the light off?"

No answer.

"Do you need your headphones?"

Romilly shouted, "STOP."

Tamsin froze. She had believed she was offering choices. To Romilly, each offer had arrived as another task.

Fictional composite case.

This is one of the hardest lessons in meltdown support: help can become load.

Meltdown Is a Capacity Problem

A meltdown is commonly described in autism guidance as an involuntary response to overwhelm rather than goal-directed misbehaviour. The National Autistic Society advises reducing sensory input, giving time and space, and remaining calm rather than attempting punishment or complex reasoning during the peak (National Autistic Society, 2020).

For a romantic partner, the word **involuntary** can be both relieving and confusing.

Does it mean nothing that happens during meltdown matters?

No.

It means you should not interpret the existence of the meltdown itself as a calculated relational strategy. It does not mean every action within the episode is harmless, nor that prevention and repair are unnecessary.

The correct sequence is:

protect → reduce → recover → review.

Protect: Safety Before Pride

Public meltdowns can create intense embarrassment for both people. The temptation is to control appearance.

“Everyone is looking.”

“Get up.”

“Stop making a scene.”

“Act normal until we get outside.”

These demands add social threat to overload.

If the environment is safe enough to leave, focus on leaving. If the person needs to sit on the floor, stim, cover their ears, cry, or move repetitively, the goal is not to make the behaviour socially pleasing.

The goal is safety.

That includes your safety.

If objects are being thrown, fists are striking walls, or the person is moving toward you aggressively, increase distance. Do not stand within reach because leaving feels unkind. If you need to move children or pets away, do it. If emergency help is needed, get it.

A nervous-system explanation does not require physical martyrdom.

Reduce: Think Subtraction

During a meltdown, partners often search for the right thing to add.

A better phrase.

A better grounding technique.

A better explanation.

A better question.

The first move is usually subtraction.

Subtract noise.

Subtract light.

Subtract people.

Subtract choices.

Subtract language.

Subtract the argument.

Subtract social demands.

Subtract touch unless requested.

Subtract urgency where possible.

This is why the Meltdown Protocol begins with reduction rather than reassurance.

The Question Paradox

Choice is usually respectful. During severe overload, choice can become work.

"What do you need?" is a broad cognitive task.

"Do you want water, headphones, the bedroom, the garden, your blanket, or for me to leave?" is six tasks.

A lower-demand approach might be:

"Water is here."

"I am turning off the main light."

"I am moving to the doorway."

"You do not need to answer."

If your partner has chosen a specific signal in advance, use it.

The point is not to take over. It is to remove the need for rapid executive decisions.

Words That Usually Cost Too Much

During peak overload, avoid:

- “Why are you doing this?”
- “You're overreacting.”
- “Use your words.”
- “I need you to communicate.”
- “You can't just shut me out.”
- “Tell me what you need.” repeated again and again.
- “Calm down.”
- “This is ridiculous.”
- “We need to finish this now.”
- “Look at me when I'm talking to you.”

Even accurate statements can be badly timed.

“You promised you would pay that bill” may be true.

It can wait.

Touch: Never Assume Comfort

Popular relationship advice often treats touch as universal reassurance.

It is not.

During sensory overload, touch may feel amplified, painful, trapping, or impossible to filter. Trauma can add another layer: a loving partner's hand may be interpreted by the nervous system as restraint or threat.

Some autistic people actively seek pressure during meltdown. They may want a weighted blanket, firm self-applied pressure, or a specific kind of contact. The important part is **chosen**.

Have the conversation while calm:

“When you are very overloaded, do you ever want touch?”

“What kind?”

"How will I know?"

"What should I never do?"

Do not use the existence of a prior yes as permanent consent. If the person recoils or says stop, stop.

The Fight About Facts

Meltdowns often occur in contexts where a real disagreement already exists.

This creates a strong temptation for the other partner to continue because stopping feels like letting dysregulation "win."

Suppose the argument concerns reckless spending.

If every financial conversation ends in meltdown, the supporting partner may fear that pausing reinforces avoidance.

The solution is to separate **timing** from **outcome**.

You can say:

"We are stopping because neither of us can do this safely now. The bill is still a problem. We will return to it tomorrow at ten."

The topic does not disappear.

The debate does.

This is a central practice in the book: **do not make nervous-system capacity responsible for deciding relationship content.**

What Recovery Looks Like

After the peak, a person may be exhausted, headachy, ashamed, hungry, tearful, quiet, physically sore, or unable to tolerate much interaction.

Recovery is not the moment for a detailed autopsy.

Allow basics first:

- water;
- food if wanted;
- bathroom;
- medication as normally prescribed;

- low sensory input;
- sleep or rest;
- familiar repetitive activity;
- solitude or quiet company according to preference.

Do not demand emotional reassurance for yourself from a person whose capacity has barely returned.

That reassurance may matter. Seek it later, or from your own support in the meantime if needed.

Shame Makes Prevention Harder

Many autistic adults describe shame after visible dysregulation. If every post-meltdown conversation begins with "You were out of control again," the person may become more motivated to hide early distress.

Hidden distress often means lost prevention time.

You want your partner to be able to say:

"I am at amber."

"I need to leave."

"I cannot do this conversation."

"Words are going."

That requires an environment where early disclosure is not mocked or treated as weakness.

Compassion after meltdown is therefore practical, not merely kind. It protects future warning signals.

But Shame Is Not Accountability

There is an opposite problem too.

A person can feel terrible after a meltdown and still avoid repairing what happened.

"I hate myself" is not the same as "I understand that I frightened you when I punched the door."

"I am the worst person alive" may actually make repair harder because the harmed partner is pushed into comforting the person who caused the harm.

Specific accountability sounds different:

"I was overloaded and lost control. I yelled inches from your face. That frightened you. I need a plan that gets me out of the room earlier, and I will replace the broken lamp."

Explanation and responsibility can coexist in one paragraph.

The Meltdown Card

Create a four-column card together.

MORE

What helps?

Examples: dark room, space, pacing, fan, weighted blanket, headphones, quiet presence.

LESS

What should be reduced?

Examples: questions, light, eye contact, touch, noise, people.

NEVER

What should the partner not do?

Examples: block the exit, restrain, follow, insist on speech, film the episode, call family members to watch.

ASK FIRST

What may help sometimes but not always?

Examples: touch, music, cold water, pressure, going outside, medication that is already prescribed for use as directed.

Keep the card short enough to use under stress.

A Different Ending to the Same Scene

Return to Tamsin and Romilly.

Romilly says, "Stop asking me questions."

This time Tamsin does not ask whether she should leave.

She turns off the overhead light because that is part of their agreed plan. She places Romilly's headphones on the edge of the table. She says one sentence.

"I am moving to the sitting room. No answer needed."

Then she goes.

Twenty-five minutes later, Romilly texts one word: "Water."

Tamsin leaves a glass outside the door.

The disagreement that preceded the meltdown is not solved.

But something else has been achieved.

They have stopped turning overload into a second crisis.

Meltdowns in Front of Other People

Public episodes create another layer of pressure because strangers, relatives, or children may react. Your instinct may be to explain your partner while they are still overwhelmed. Usually, reduce the audience first.

A short sentence is enough: "They need space. Please step back."

Do not disclose trauma history or diagnostic details without permission merely to make observers understand. Privacy remains important during distress.

If family members crowd in with advice, assign one person to clear the area rather than allowing five helpers to ask questions. If staff are involved, communicate the practical need: quieter space, fewer people, time, a clear exit. You do not need to deliver an autism lecture while your partner is overloaded.

Afterward, the autistic partner may feel embarrassed. Avoid turning the event into evidence that they should never go out again. Review what made the environment hard and what would make future participation safer. Sometimes the answer is shorter attendance, quieter venues, advance information, or not attending. Sometimes the answer is simply that an unusually bad day occurred.

The aim is not to make meltdowns invisible so other people remain comfortable. It is to make support more effective while preserving dignity.

What You Do With Your Own Adrenaline

During someone else's meltdown, your body may enter fight, flight, freeze, or appeasement. You can understand intellectually that the episode is overload and still feel threatened by volume, movement, or unpredictability.

Prepare a partner protocol too.

If you tend to fight, your risk may be shouting back, arguing, or moving closer. Your plan may be to step toward an exit, lower your own voice, and use one sentence only.

If you tend to pursue, your risk may be questions and following. Your plan may be to put your phone down, move to the agreed room, and wait for the return signal.

If you freeze, your risk may be staying in an unsafe space because you cannot decide what to do. Your plan may be written and simple: **keys, phone, children, outside**.

If you appease, your risk may be agreeing to things you do not mean in order to stop distress. Your plan may be: **no decisions during the episode**.

Your regulation matters because co-regulation is impossible when you are also beyond capacity. Sometimes the best support you can provide is distance.

The autistic partner's meltdown is not proof that you should have no nervous-system response of your own. The skill is noticing your response early enough that it does not become a second escalation.

Chapter 6: When Overload Moves Inward

Arden Blythe had two defensible options and enough evidence to rule out neither.

His partner, Elowen Blake, had stopped speaking in the middle of a serious conversation about childcare. Elowen was sitting at the end of the bed, looking at the floor. Arden could interpret the silence as shutdown and give space. Or he could interpret it as avoidance and insist that a parent cannot simply disappear from a necessary discussion.

Both concerns were real.

The mistake would be trying to solve both at the same time.

Fictional composite case.

Shutdown teaches a difficult relationship skill: **protect incapacity now, address avoidance later if it exists.**

Quiet Can Be a High-Distress State

A meltdown announces itself more visibly. Shutdown may not.

From the outside, a person can look calm while internally overwhelmed. NHS-linked autism guidance describes shutdown as a response to excessive information or anxiety in which communication may become difficult or stop (Leicestershire Partnership NHS Trust, n.d.).

Partners often find this harder than they expect.

Silence creates empty space, and the mind fills empty space quickly.

They hate me.

They don't care.

They are punishing me.

They are leaving.

They know they are wrong.

I have to get an answer.

Then the pursuit begins.

The Pursuit-Shutdown Loop

The loop is simple.

One partner loses language or processing capacity.

The other partner becomes frightened by the loss of contact.

Fear produces more questions.

More questions produce more demand.

More demand deepens shutdown.

Deeper shutdown increases the other partner's fear.

Both people can feel abandoned in the same room.

This loop is not solved by deciding whose nervous system is more legitimate.

It is solved by a communication bridge that requires less capacity.

First, Rule Out What Should Not Be Assumed

A familiar shutdown pattern may be recognisable to a couple. A new or unusual loss of responsiveness should not automatically be labelled autistic shutdown.

If the person loses consciousness, has signs of stroke or seizure, has taken substances, has been injured, has severe breathing difficulty, shows new confusion, or appears medically unwell, seek appropriate medical help.

Psychological labels should not delay medical assessment when something is different enough to raise concern.

Reduce the Bandwidth

Conversation has a bandwidth requirement.

Consider this question:

"Can you tell me why you felt I was being unfair when I asked you to change the school pickup schedule, and what you think we should do instead?"

That question requires memory, language, emotional processing, perspective-taking, sequencing, decision-making, and response formulation.

Now compare:

"Words hard?"

A nod may answer.

Then:

"Text later?"

Another nod.

Bandwidth has been reduced without treating the person like a child.

Low-bandwidth communication is adult communication adapted to current capacity.

The Shutdown Ladder

Create a hierarchy from highest to lowest demand.

Level 5: Normal spoken conversation

Full sentences, discussion, problem-solving.

Level 4: Short spoken responses

One question at a time. Short answers.

Level 3: Binary communication

Yes/no. Thumbs. Two-card choices.

Level 2: Written or symbolic communication

Text, note, coloured card, pre-written phrase.

Level 1: No-response-needed information

"I am in the living room. Water is here. We will not discuss this tonight."

Level 0: Quiet safety

No communication demand beyond what safety requires.

The goal is not always to climb the ladder immediately. Sometimes Level 0 is where recovery happens.

The Return Signal Protects Both People

The return signal is one of the most powerful devices in the book because it solves two different problems at once.

For the shut-down partner, it removes pressure to explain.

For the waiting partner, it reduces relational ambiguity.

A good return signal contains three pieces of information:

13. **State:** "No words."
14. **Relationship:** "Not leaving / not ending us / safe."
15. **Return:** "Text at 8 / talk tomorrow / check in after sleep."

Examples:

> **NO WORDS. SAFE. TEXT 8 P.M.**
>
> **SHUTDOWN. NOT A BREAKUP. TOMORROW 10 A.M.**
>
> **CAN'T PROCESS. PLEASE STOP QUESTIONS. I WILL RETURN.**

The wording should fit the couple. A card is useful because the person does not have to invent language when language is least available.

What If They Miss the Return Time?

This is where support becomes relationship work.

If the return time passes occasionally because recovery took longer, update the plan.

A one-word message—"later"—may be enough if that was agreed.

If the person repeatedly uses shutdown to postpone difficult subjects for days or weeks with no reliable return, the problem has changed.

You still should not force speech during shutdown.

You should address the **pattern of non-return** when both people are regulated.

Possible boundaries include:

- important financial decisions cannot remain unresolved indefinitely;
- parenting responsibilities need an agreed process even when one parent shuts down;
- a conflict pause must include a new meeting time within a set range;
- written communication may replace spoken discussion;
- couples therapy may be needed if all serious subjects collapse.

"No capacity now" and "no responsibility ever" are not the same statement.

Stonewalling and Shutdown Are Not Identical

Stonewalling is a relationship behaviour involving withdrawal from interaction. It can arise for many reasons, including overwhelm, conflict avoidance, hostility, or a learned coping pattern. Shutdown describes a state of reduced capacity under overwhelm.

The two can overlap, but they should not be assumed identical.

Useful questions after the fact include:

- Was speech genuinely difficult or inaccessible?
- Did other abilities also reduce?
- Did sensory load or cumulative stress precede the silence?
- Did the person use a lower-bandwidth form of connection if available?
- Did they return to the subject later?
- Was silence used to create fear or control?
- Does the pattern occur mainly under overload, or whenever accountability is requested?

Intent is not always easy to infer. Pattern and follow-through matter more.

The Supporting Partner's Abandonment Alarm

If silence is difficult for you, do not shame yourself for reacting.

Human attachment systems care about contact. If you have your own trauma history, unexplained withdrawal may be especially activating.

But your fear cannot make speech compulsory for someone who has lost access to it.

You need your own regulation plan.

It may include:

- texting a friend rather than repeatedly texting your partner;
- writing down what you want to say and waiting;
- going for a walk;
- using your own grounding practice;
- reminding yourself of the return signal;
- sleeping separately if the unresolved tension is too activating;
- contacting your therapist or support person when the pattern is severe.

The relationship becomes more stable when neither person's emergency response is allowed to run the whole interaction.

Do Not Turn Silence Into a Courtroom

When speech returns, the waiting partner may have prepared a case.

"First, you ignored me. Then you walked away. Then you left me alone for three hours. Do you understand how cruel that is?"

If the person was genuinely in shutdown, beginning with accusation may trigger shame, defensiveness, or another loss of capacity.

Try separating observation from impact:

"You stopped speaking around seven. You texted the card at seven-fifteen and came back at nine-thirty. I was frightened at first, and the card helped. I still need us to finish the childcare decision."

This sentence does not pretend the waiting was easy.

It also does not misname incapacity as cruelty.

Written Communication Is Not Second-Class Communication

Mixed-neurotype couples sometimes treat spoken emotional conversation as the gold standard and writing as a compromise.

That assumption deserves examination.

Research around the double empathy problem challenges one-sided models in which communication failure is located only in the autistic person. Studies show that misunderstanding can be reciprocal across neurotypes and that interaction quality depends partly on fit between communication styles (Jones et al., 2024).

If writing allows both people to be clearer, slower, and less reactive, then writing may be the better medium for some discussions.

A texted apology can be sincere.

A shared document can be a real relationship conversation.

A written agenda can prevent overload.

A voice note can sit between text and live speech.

The goal is mutual understanding, not performance of a preferred communication format.

Returning to Arden and Elowen

Arden decides not to force the childcare discussion during shutdown.

He places the agreed card on the bed: **NO TALK NEEDED. CHILDCARE DECISION STILL OPEN. TEXT BY NOON TOMORROW.**

Elowen turns the card over. On the back are three printed options:

> **A. I can text tonight.**
>
> **B. I can text tomorrow morning.**
>
> **C. I need you to choose this week, but I will take the next decision.**

Elowen points to B.

The couple has not solved childcare.

They have solved the more immediate problem: how to preserve both capacity and responsibility.

That distinction is the bridge from shutdown back to partnership.

What Shutdown Can Do to Intimacy

Repeated shutdown does not only affect arguments. It can alter the emotional climate of the relationship. The waiting partner may stop raising vulnerable subjects because the anticipated silence feels too painful. The shut-down partner may start avoiding closeness because closeness predicts demands they fear they cannot meet. Sexual contact may become difficult if unresolved conflict accumulates. Small misunderstandings can remain open for days because neither person trusts the re-entry process.

This is why the return signal is not a minor accommodation. It protects intimacy from becoming hostage to verbal capacity.

Couples can also create **levels of return**. A full discussion may still be impossible, but a partial return can occur:

"Still low words. I read your message. I understand the decision matters. Full answer tomorrow."

That small contact prevents the waiting partner from having to choose between total pursuit and total uncertainty.

If shutdown frequently lasts for very long periods, causes major functional impairment, or has changed markedly from the person's usual pattern, seek professional assessment rather than assuming every episode is simply an expected autistic response. Severe depression, trauma-related dissociation, medical illness, medication effects, and other conditions can also affect responsiveness.

The book's rule remains the same: support the state you can observe, but do not use the label to close investigation.

Long Shutdowns and Practical Life

A short shutdown may allow the world to wait. A long one may collide with work, childcare, medication, travel, or urgent decisions. The couple needs a practical plan for the minimum information that must still move.

Create an **essential-only channel**. It might permit messages about children, medical needs, transport, immediate money, or safety while postponing emotional processing.

Examples:

"School pickup changed to 4:00. No reply needed unless you cannot do it."

"Your medication is on the table."

"I need yes/no by noon: can you take the dog to the vet?"

Do not smuggle relationship arguments into the essential channel. “The children need dinner, unlike some people who remember their responsibilities” defeats the purpose.

If long shutdowns are common, the household may also need backup systems: shared calendars, automatic payments, written childcare instructions, emergency contacts, and clear task ownership. These are not romantic, but they reduce the number of urgent verbal demands placed on a person whose language may periodically disappear.

Practical resilience protects the relationship from making every shutdown an operational emergency.

Chapter 7: When the Past Feels Present

The room was quiet except for the click of the radiator.

Marlowe Quinn was sitting on the floor beside the bed. Her partner, Wren Hollis, was standing by the wardrobe with both hands clenched around the sleeves of her jumper.

Marlowe had raised her voice once.

Not screamed. Not threatened. Raised it.

Wren had stopped seeing the room as a disagreement between two adults in 2026. Her body was responding to a different room, a different voice, and a different person who had once made leaving impossible.

Marlowe understood one thing immediately: proving that she was not that person would not work if she kept standing between Wren and the door.

She moved.

Fictional composite case.

A Flashback Is a Present-Tense Experience of Past Threat

PTSD is not simply having painful memories. Trauma-related re-experiencing can include intrusive memories, nightmares, and flashbacks in which elements of the traumatic event are experienced with a strong sense of happening again. The World Health Organization describes PTSD around re-experiencing, avoidance, and a persistent perception of current threat; the VA similarly describes flashbacks as feeling as though the trauma is happening again (WHO, 2024b; VA, n.d.-a).

That distinction matters to partners.

If your loved one is remembering the past while remaining firmly oriented to the present, ordinary supportive conversation may be possible.

If their nervous system is responding as though the past is present, reasoning about the relationship may have very little effect until orientation returns.

The useful question becomes:

What helps the current room become the current room again?

Do Not Begin by Arguing With the Fear

A frightened person says, "You're trapping me."

You know the door is open.

Your first impulse may be correction.

"I am not trapping you. Don't accuse me of that."

The factual correction may be true. It may also miss the state.

A more useful first move is behavioural:

step away from the doorway.

Then use a factual cue:

"The door is open. You can leave."

The difference is small in language and large in nervous-system terms.

One sentence asks the frightened person to update their interpretation.

The other changes the environment so updating becomes easier.

Grounding Means Connecting With Now

The VA's guidance for flashbacks includes orienting to the present place and year, looking around, moving, drinking water, and contacting trusted support (VA, n.d.-a). Grounding is not magic. It is a family of strategies that help attention reconnect with current sensory, temporal, and relational information.

For autistic people, grounding must be personalised carefully.

Many common grounding lists assume that more sensory input is automatically helpful:

find five things you can see;

hold ice;

smell something strong;

splash cold water;

have someone touch your shoulders.

For a person already near sensory overload, those instructions may be intolerable.

A better question is:

Which present-time cues are regulating for this nervous system?

Build a Grounding Menu Before You Need It

Do not invent the menu during crisis.

Discuss it when both people are calm.

Possible categories include:

Place cues

- reading the current address;
- looking at a familiar object that did not exist during the trauma;
- noticing a recent photograph;
- seeing the current date on a phone or card;
- opening the door and looking outside.

Body cues

- feet pressed into the floor;
- slow walking;
- holding a familiar fabric;
- sitting with back against a wall;
- rocking;
- placing one's own hand on the chest or thigh;
- drinking water.

Time cues

- “It is 2026.”
- “You are thirty-nine.”
- “The event ended years ago.”
- “Today is Tuesday.”

Relationship cues

- the current partner says their own name;
- the partner states what they will not do: "I will not touch you."
- the partner states freedom: "You can leave this room."
- a pre-written card reminds the person of chosen facts.

Choice cues

- "Door open or closed?"
- "Me here or outside?"
- "Light on or lamp only?"

Choice can restore a sense of agency, but only if the person has enough capacity to choose. If choice becomes another demand, reduce it.

When the Partner Is the Reminder

This can be deeply painful.

You may be a loving partner who suddenly sees fear in the other person's facc as thcy look at you.

You may hear your name mixed with someone else's.

You may be told, "Don't hit me," when you have never hit them.

Your own nervous system may react with hurt, anger, or urgency to defend yourself.

There will be time for that hurt.

During the flashback, your task is not to win acquittal.

Do what makes present safety more obvious:

increase distance;

lower your voice;

sit rather than loom if sitting is safer;

keep exits open;

state what you are doing before you do it;

avoid sudden touch;

end the argument.

Later, you may need space to process what it felt like to be seen as dangerous.

Partners need care too.

Do Not Force Trauma Disclosure

A flashback may make you curious because understanding the memory seems like the route to prevention.

Do not interrogate.

“What happened to you?”

“Was it your father?”

“What did he do when the door closed?”

“Why have you never told me this?”

These questions may turn support into pressure and can move the partner into a role that properly belongs to trauma therapy.

Evidence-based PTSD treatments include trauma-focused psychotherapies such as Cognitive Processing Therapy, Prolonged Exposure, and EMDR. These are structured clinical treatments, not techniques for spouses to improvise at home (VA, n.d.-b). Research and clinician consensus on adapting trauma work for autistic people also indicate that therapists may need to adjust communication, pacing, sensory conditions, and other aspects of delivery (Fisher et al., 2023).

Your job is not to process the trauma memory.

Your job is to be a safe current person.

“Emotional Flashback”: Use the Term Carefully

In popular CPTSD writing, you may encounter the phrase **emotional flashback** to describe sudden states of fear, shame, helplessness, or abandonment that feel connected to earlier trauma without vivid visual memory.

Many readers find the phrase useful. It is not, however, a separate formal diagnostic category in ICD-11 or DSM terminology. In this book, when such states are discussed, they are treated as a descriptive way some survivors understand trauma activation—not as something a partner should diagnose on sight.

This caution matters because ordinary strong emotion should not automatically become evidence of trauma.

Sometimes your partner is simply angry with you.

Sometimes the relationship issue is real.

The flashback protocol does not abolish disagreement. It changes the order of operations when past threat appears to be dominating the present.

The Trauma Trigger and the Real Problem Can Coexist

Suppose you say:

"We need to talk about the fact that you hid £2,000 of debt."

Your partner's childhood involved severe punishment around money. The discussion triggers intense fear and a flashback.

The trauma response deserves care.

The hidden debt remains real.

After the episode, the couple must return to the money problem.

This is where many trauma-affected relationships become stuck. The supporting partner fears that any return to the issue will trigger the trauma again, so the issue disappears. Or the supporting partner becomes so determined not to "enable" avoidance that they force the conversation at the worst possible moment.

The alternative is planned re-entry.

Maybe the discussion happens with a therapist.

Maybe it begins in writing.

Maybe it is divided into factual and emotional parts.

Maybe the trauma survivor practices grounding before the meeting.

Maybe the couple schedules breaks.

What you do not do is confuse immediate stabilisation with permanent exemption.

Flashback or Current Danger?

Trauma can produce false alarms.

Trauma can also sharpen awareness of real danger.

If your partner says they feel unsafe, do not automatically tell them it is their trauma.

Ask what is happening in the present.

Are you yelling?

Are you blocking the exit?

Have you been drinking?

Are you refusing to let them end sex?

Are you threatening to take money, children, housing, or immigration status?

Is there current intimidation?

The phrase "you're triggered" can itself become a form of dismissal if it is used to avoid looking at present behaviour.

The Flashback Protocol only works ethically when current safety is taken seriously.

Create the Back-to-Now Card

A personalised card might read:

MY NAME: Wren Hollis.

TODAY: Tuesday, 18 August 2026.

WHERE I AM: Home.

WHAT IS TRUE NOW: The bedroom door opens from the inside. I have my phone. I can leave the room. Marlowe will not touch me unless I ask.

WHAT HELPS: lamp only, feet on floor, dog beside me, no questions for ten minutes.

WHAT DOES NOT HELP: being hugged, cold water, repeated reassurance, being asked what memory I am having.

The card is not universal. It is an agreement.

The Sentence That Makes Space for Both People

After the flashback, when enough capacity has returned, try this structure:

> **"What happened in your nervous system was real. What happened in our relationship also matters."**

Then discuss them separately.

First: what reminder, grounding, or safety adjustment was relevant?

Second: what disagreement, boundary, or repair remains?

Trauma needs compassion.

A relationship needs reality.

Neither should be sacrificed to the other.

Nightmares, Sleep, and the Partner Beside You

Trauma-related nightmares create a special problem because the supporting partner may be pulled into dysregulation before either person is fully awake. The trauma survivor may wake disoriented, frightened, defensive, or unable to tolerate touch. The partner may instinctively grab, shake, hug, or ask what happened.

Plan for nights while awake.

Ask whether waking touch is welcome. Some people want their name spoken from a distance before any contact. Others prefer the light left off. Some need to sit up and orient visually. Some want the door open. Some need water. Some want no questions until morning.

If nightmares are frequent, severe, or worsening, they belong in clinical care rather than being managed only through a partner protocol. Sleep loss can also lower autistic sensory tolerance the following day, creating a cycle in which trauma-related sleep disturbance increases the risk of overload.

A couple can respond to that interaction pragmatically. The morning after a severe nightmare may not be the time for an optional crowded event or a major relationship meeting. That is not surrender to trauma. It is recognition that baseline capacity has changed.

The Moment Map works best when you understand that states do not end at the bedroom door. What happens at night can shape the threshold of the next day.

Trauma Activation Around Touch and Sex

Physical intimacy can contain some of the strongest past-to-present cues in a relationship. A particular position, smell, phrase, pressure, pace, or feeling of being unable to stop may activate threat even in a consensual relationship. Autism can add sensory variables that change from day to day.

Do not treat a trauma response during sex as a communication failure to solve while continuing sexual contact. Stop. Create physical choice. Ask the minimum needed to establish consent and safety.

A useful calm-time plan can include:

- a word or gesture that means immediate stop;
- agreement that freezing counts as a reason to pause rather than as consent;
- types of touch that are never used without explicit request;
- lighting and sensory preferences;
- whether verbal check-ins help or disrupt;
- what kind of aftercare is welcome;
- whether a trauma-triggering sexual issue belongs in therapy before the couple tries it again.

Consent is not a therapeutic exercise. A partner should never continue unwanted contact because they believe avoidance must be challenged for PTSD recovery. Trauma-focused exposure is clinical work carried out within a treatment plan, not a rationale for overriding sexual boundaries.

The strongest intimate relationships make stopping safe.

Chapter 8: When You Cannot Tell

What should you do when every explanation is plausible and none is reliable?

Elowen Blake faced that question at two in the morning.

Her partner, Sloane Everly, had awakened abruptly after a nightmare. The smoke alarm in the hallway had begun chirping because of a low battery. Sloane covered her ears, pushed past Elowen, started crying, then froze beside the front door. She could not answer whether she was awake enough to know where she was. When Elowen moved closer, Sloane recoiled.

Was this sensory overload?

A trauma flashback?

A shutdown emerging after panic?

All three?

Elowen did not need a diagnosis at two in the morning.

She needed a low-risk next move.

Fictional composite case.

Uncertainty Is Not Failure

The most dangerous promise a book like this could make is that you will learn to identify every episode correctly.

You will not.

Neither will your partner always know in the moment.

Trauma and autism research gives good reason for humility. Autistic adults report high trauma exposure and PTSD symptoms, and clinical literature describes overlap and diagnostic overshadowing (Andrzejewski et al., 2024; Kildahl & Helverschou, 2024). Add sleep loss, anxiety, burnout, pain, medication effects, relationship conflict, and ordinary human variation, and real-time certainty becomes unrealistic.

The Mixed/Unclear Protocol is therefore not the "other" category.

It is the protocol for mature uncertainty.

The Common-Denominator Response

When you do not know whether the dominant process is meltdown, shutdown, or trauma activation, begin with actions that are unlikely to make any of them worse.

Keep people physically safe

Create distance from danger. Keep exits available. Remove children from frightening scenes. Move dangerous objects when you can do so safely.

Stop the argument

Do not continue relationship problem-solving while the state is unclear and capacity is visibly impaired.

Reduce sensory input

Lower noise, light, crowding, and movement.

Reduce verbal demand

Use fewer words. Stop repeated questions.

Offer one gentle present-time cue

"We are at home. The argument is paused. You do not have to answer."

Offer simple agency if possible

"Space or quiet company?"

Avoid surprise touch

Touch can intensify both sensory overload and trauma threat.

Observe rather than label

Notice what helps.

This is the core of the Mixed/Unclear Protocol.

Why "Grounding" Can Backfire in Overload

Suppose your partner is primarily overloaded.

You begin a grounding exercise:

"Name five things you can see."

No response.

"Come on, look at me. Five things."

Now you are adding visual search, language production, performance demand, and eye-contact pressure.

A technique that is useful in one state has become load in another.

The mixed protocol therefore uses **one low-demand orientation cue** rather than a full exercise unless the person has asked for more.

If your partner responds well, continue gently.

If not, go quieter.

Why Complete Withdrawal Can Backfire in Trauma

Now consider the opposite error.

You assume overload and leave without explanation.

Your partner is actually in intense abandonment-related trauma activation. Your sudden disappearance becomes more threatening.

The mixed protocol again gives a middle route.

"I am going to the chair by the door. I will stay quiet."

Or:

"I am stepping into the hallway. The door stays open. You can text me."

Presence can be reduced without becoming disappearance.

Space or Quiet Company?

This two-option question is one of the most useful in the book.

Space or quiet company?

It acknowledges two common needs without demanding a detailed explanation.

If the person cannot choose, use the agreed default.

Perhaps the default is:

partner steps back six feet and stays visible;

or partner leaves the room but sends one text after ten minutes;

or partner remains silent in the next room with the door open.

The best default is personal.

Stop Naming the State at the Person

A distressed person says, “Leave me alone.”

You answer, “You're having a trauma response.”

They say, “No, I'm not.”

You answer, “You can't see it because you're dysregulated.”

Now the framework has become unfalsifiable. Whatever the person says is used as evidence that you understand them better than they understand themselves.

Do not do this.

Use the map privately to guide your behaviour.

Speak observationally:

“Words seem hard.”

“I am reducing noise.”

“We are pausing.”

“I won't touch you.”

“We can decide what this was later.”

A good framework reduces power struggles. It should not create a new one.

The Pattern May Change Mid-Episode

A mixed episode can move.

A trauma reminder triggers fear.

Fear increases sensory sensitivity.

The person begins pacing and shouting.

The partner talks more in an attempt to reassure.

Language demand becomes intolerable.

The autistic person melts down.

Afterward, they shut down.

Which protocol applies?

The answer can change over time.

Early: open exit and orient to safety.

Peak: reduce all input and protect physical space.

Later: stop requiring speech and allow recovery.

The Moment Map is a map, not a stamp. Reorient when the terrain changes.

The Lowest-Risk Sentence

If you remember only one sentence for unclear moments, use:

> **"We don't have to work out what this is right now."**

Then add one action:

"I am turning the light down."

"I am moving back."

"I am stopping the argument."

"You do not need to answer."

This sentence removes the diagnostic demand and the relationship demand at once.

Mixed Does Not Mean Meaningless

After recovery, mixed episodes often teach more than clean ones because they show how different loads interact.

Review in layers.

Layer 1: Baseline capacity

Sleep, illness, burnout, hunger, pain.

Layer 2: Autistic load

Noise, social demand, uncertainty, change, communication complexity.

Layer 3: Trauma load

Reminders, anniversaries, relational cues, threat meanings.

Layer 4: Partner interaction

Questions, pursuit, touch, tone, leaving, arguing, reassurance.

Layer 5: Recovery

What helped first?

This layered review is far more useful than asking, "So was it autism or trauma?"

Build an If-We-Don't-Know Plan

Write the following together:

If we cannot tell what is happening, we will:

16. Stop the conflict.
17. Keep exits open.
18. Reduce light/noise/people.
19. Use no more than one short sentence at a time.
20. Avoid touch unless requested.
21. Use the phrase "space or quiet company?"
22. Follow our default if no answer is possible.
23. Delay interpretation.

24. Review after recovery.

Then add:

Our default quiet-company position is: ________

Our default check-in time is: ________

The present-time cue that usually helps is: ________

The sensory changes that usually help are: ________

The things we should never do are: ________

The plan works because it is simple enough to remember when both people are stressed.

Returning to Two in the Morning

Elowen removes the chirping smoke alarm from the hallway and closes it in the utility room until the battery can be replaced safely. She leaves the hall light off. She does not touch Sloane.

She says:

"You are home. I am by the stairs. No answer needed."

Then she waits.

Sloane begins rocking. After several minutes she whispers, "Door."

Elowen opens the front door a few inches and steps back.

Fresh night air enters.

The episode does not become neat. Elowen still cannot tell whether the nightmare, alarm, sensory pain, or trauma memory mattered most.

She does not need to.

She has found the next safe move.

Your Own Uncertainty Needs a Protocol

The Mixed/Unclear Protocol reduces the diagnosed partner's load, but the supporting partner also needs a way to tolerate not knowing.

Uncertainty can produce compulsive interpretation. You search online while the episode is still happening. You replay the last sentence. You decide that if you can name the state, you can make the relationship safe.

Try a three-line self-protocol:

What I know: "Speech is reduced, the room is loud, and my partner is backing away."

What I do not know: "I do not know whether trauma or overload is dominant."

What I can do: "I can stop talking, lower the noise, move away from the doorway, and wait."

This structure keeps uncertainty from becoming helplessness.

It also prevents you from borrowing certainty from internet labels that may not fit your partner. The more emotionally charged the relationship moment, the more attractive a confident explanation can feel. A modest response based on observable facts is often safer than a sophisticated explanation based on guesswork.

If later review repeatedly fails because neither person can make sense of episodes, bring examples to an autism- and trauma-informed clinician. A partner is allowed to reach the limit of home interpretation.

A Mixed-State Conflict From Beginning to End

Carys has worked late. She arrives home hungry and overstimulated. Briar has been waiting to discuss a message from Carys's former partner about a legal matter. The message itself is a trauma reminder. Briar begins with, "We need to deal with this tonight."

Carys says, "Not now."

Briar hears avoidance and presses. Carys's speech becomes repetitive. The kitchen light is buzzing. Briar steps closer because she wants reassurance that Carys is listening. Carys backs toward the door and begins saying, "Don't block me."

At this point, several processes may be active.

The mixed protocol changes the scene. Briar steps away from the door, turns off the light, and says, “The message can wait. I am not blocking you. No answer needed.”

Carys leaves the kitchen and sits on the stairs. Briar remains in the living room rather than following. Ten minutes later Carys texts, “Too much. Also scared. Tomorrow.”

The next day, they review the layers. Hunger and sensory overload lowered capacity. The legal message carried trauma threat. Briar's urgency added verbal demand. Standing near the door amplified the threat cue.

No single label would have produced a better plan than this layered account. Their revision is concrete: legal messages are never discussed immediately after work; the kitchen light is replaced; and either partner may use “tomorrow” once, provided a return time is set.

That is what the mixed category is for: not indecision, but multi-cause accuracy.

Chapter 9: Safety Comes Before Interpretation

The language available to couples has changed. Today we have terms for autistic overload, trauma responses, sensory needs, and relationship safety that can help people describe patterns that once remained unnamed or misunderstood.

Better language creates one risk of its own: we can become so interested in explanation that we fail to name danger.

The sentence **"they were dysregulated"** can be true and still be incomplete.

This chapter is about the missing half.

Safety Is Not a Judgment About Character

When a partner says, "I need to leave the room because I am afraid," the first task is not to determine whether the frightened interpretation is perfectly fair.

Fear is data.

So is blocked movement.

So are thrown objects.

So are threats.

So is a child hiding in a bedroom because arguments have become frightening.

You do not have to decide that your partner is a monster in order to make a safety plan.

You do not have to decide that every frightening event was intentional.

You only have to take current risk seriously.

Dysregulation and Abuse Are Different Questions

Abuse is not defined by diagnosis. It involves patterns of behaviour that create coercion, control, fear, or harm. An autistic person can be abused. An autistic person can also be abusive. A trauma survivor can be abused. A trauma survivor can also abuse others.

The existence of meltdown, shutdown, PTSD, or CPTSD does not settle the question.

Likewise, a frightening-looking meltdown is not automatically a pattern of coercive control.

A person who screams incoherently under sensory overload and later works actively to prevent recurrence is not necessarily using the episode to dominate a partner. A person who deliberately blocks exits, controls money, threatens custody, monitors communications, or uses fear to obtain compliance presents a different relational pattern.

Sometimes the same relationship contains both dysregulation and abuse. That is why the categories must not be collapsed.

Non-Negotiable Safety Lines

Every couple should be able to state certain boundaries before the next episode.

Examples:

- No hitting, kicking, choking, biting, or throwing objects at another person.
- No blocking exits.
- No dangerous driving during conflict.
- No sexual contact without consent.
- No threats to harm self or others as a means of forcing compliance.
- No weapons introduced into arguments.
- No destroying another person's essential belongings.
- No frightening children as an accepted cost of adult dysregulation.
- No preventing someone from contacting help.

The exact plan depends on the household, but the principle does not: **dysregulation does not eliminate the other person's right to safety.**

"But They Can't Control It"

This sentence often appears when discussing meltdown.

The loss of behavioural control may indeed be involuntary.

Safety planning still matters.

Consider epilepsy. A seizure is involuntary. That does not mean a person with uncontrolled seizures should drive without regard to risk. The analogy is imperfect, but the logic is useful: involuntary events can still require prevention, environmental change, professional care, and limits around hazardous situations.

If a person's meltdowns repeatedly involve dangerous behaviour, the couple needs more than compassion in the moment.

They need prevention work.

Medical and mental health review may be appropriate.

The environment may need change.

The person may need an earlier exit strategy.

Children may need a separate safety plan.

The partner may need somewhere to go.

Repeated dangerous episodes are a systems problem, not a private test of devotion.

The Difference Between Leaving and Abandoning

Trauma survivors may experience a partner leaving the room as abandonment.

That feeling can be real.

If staying places you at risk, you still leave.

You can communicate without surrendering safety:

“I am leaving because objects are being thrown. I will contact you when it is safe.”

“I am taking the children to my sister's tonight. We can discuss next steps tomorrow.”

“I will not stay in a room where I am being threatened.”

A boundary describes your action. It does not require the other person to agree with your interpretation.

What About Self-Harm Threats?

This is especially difficult for partners.

A traumatised person may express genuine suicidal thoughts or self-harm urges. These require serious professional attention.

At the same time, a relationship can become coercive if one partner learns that threatening self-harm prevents the other from leaving, setting a boundary, or ending the relationship.

You are not qualified or obligated to manage acute suicide risk alone.

If your partner expresses imminent intent, has a plan, has taken steps toward self-harm, or you believe immediate danger is present, involve appropriate emergency or crisis professionals in your location. Do not bargain away your boundaries in exchange for a promise of safety.

The caring response is to bring in the level of support the risk requires.

Property Destruction Is Not "Just Things"

Some partners minimise broken objects because no person was hit.

Context matters. Accidentally knocking over a lamp while escaping sensory overload is not the same as smashing the partner's phone while threatening them.

But repeated property destruction can still create fear even when objects are not thrown directly at a person.

Ask:

What was broken?

Where was the other person?

Was destruction directed at items that mattered to them?

Was it used to intimidate?

Were children present?

Did the person take responsibility afterward?

Was a prevention plan made?

Has the pattern escalated?

Fear in the home deserves attention.

Children Change the Threshold

Adults can choose to remain in difficult relationships. Children cannot choose the nervous systems that organise their home.

A child who repeatedly witnesses screaming, threats, violence, dangerous property destruction, or prolonged terror is affected whether the adult behaviour is explained by autism, trauma, substance use, or something else.

A family safety plan should identify:

- where children go during an episode;
- which adult remains responsible for them;
- whether they know they are not responsible for calming a parent;
- who can be contacted;
- what situations require leaving the home;
- what professional support is needed.

Do not train children to become tiny co-regulators.

Accountability Without Humiliation

After a dangerous episode, the responsible conversation should be concrete.

Avoid global shame:

“You are terrifying.”

“You are exactly like your father.”

“You are a monster.”

Prefer specific impact and required change:

“You threw a mug toward the wall while I was beside it. I was afraid I could be hit. I will leave the room immediately if objects are thrown again. We need a prevention plan before another financial discussion.”

If the person responds with shame, keep returning to behaviour.

"I am not asking you to hate yourself. I am asking you to help make this safe."

When Couples Work Is Not Enough

Relationship communication tools are not the correct primary intervention for every situation.

If coercive control or violence is present, joint sessions can sometimes be unsafe or inappropriate because disclosures may lead to retaliation or the abusive partner may use therapeutic language to gain more control. Individual professional advice from services competent in intimate partner violence is important.

If the danger is primarily uncontrolled dysregulation rather than coercive abuse, the couple may still need individual clinical support, environmental assessment, medication review where relevant, trauma treatment, occupational therapy, or autism-informed mental health care.

The point is not to fit every safety problem into couples communication.

Your Non-Negotiable Safety Lines Exercise

Complete these sentences privately first.

I will leave the immediate space if: ________

I will take children/pets with me if: ________

I will contact emergency/professional help if: ________

I will not negotiate about: ________

The safe place I can go is: ________

The person I can contact is: ________

The items I need accessible are: phone, keys, medication, documents, money, other ________

Then, if the relationship is safe enough for collaborative planning, discuss the plan while calm.

A safety boundary is not a punishment for being autistic or traumatised.

It is the condition under which compassion remains possible.

The Chapter's Practical Judgment

When behaviour is frightening, do not ask first, "Which diagnosis explains this?"

Ask:

> **What keeps people safe?**

Then, after safety exists, interpretation can resume.

The Moment Map is a map for dysregulation.

It is not a reason to stay in danger.

Safety After the Incident

The period after a frightening event can create pressure to restore normality too quickly. The person who became dysregulated may feel ashamed and want reassurance that nothing has changed. The frightened partner may want to believe the event was exceptional. Both may agree to "move on" before a real prevention plan exists.

A safer review asks concrete questions:

- What made the event dangerous?
- What was the earliest point at which someone could have left?
- Were exits available?
- Were children or pets exposed?
- Was alcohol or another substance involved?
- Did the person recognise early warning signs?
- What professional input is now needed?
- What boundary applies if the behaviour repeats?

Documenting important incidents privately can also help a partner see patterns that are hard to recognise when each episode is followed by apology and relief. Record dates, observable behaviour, injuries or damage, and what happened afterward. Do not use records to threaten or humiliate. Use them to maintain reality.

If you find yourself deleting evidence, hiding events from friends, making excuses for injuries, or changing your behaviour primarily because you fear your partner's reaction, take those signs seriously. The question may have moved beyond dysregulation management.

Safety becomes real when it is built before the next crisis, not promised afterward.

Preserve Practical Independence

A supporting partner's safety is easier to protect when they retain practical options. This is not an instruction to prepare secretly for separation in every difficult relationship. It is a reminder that adult autonomy matters.

Know how to access your own identification, medication, phone, transport, and money. Maintain contact with people outside the relationship. Understand major household finances. Do not allow every friendship to disappear because social contact upsets your partner.

For people whose partner becomes controlling during trauma activation or dysregulation, practical dependence can make boundaries impossible to use. “I will leave if you block the door” is not an effective plan if you have no keys, no money, no person to call, and nowhere you can safely go.

If the relationship is healthy, basic independence should not be threatening. Both adults benefit from knowing how the household works and being able to function if the other becomes ill or unavailable.

Safety is partly psychological. It is also logistical.

Part III: After the Nervous System Settles

Chapter 10: Recover, Reconnect, Review, Revise

Carys Monroe used to believe that the responsible thing was to talk immediately.

If an argument ended in meltdown or shutdown, she waited until her partner looked calmer and began the debrief.

"Okay. Can we talk about what just happened?"

The sentence sounded reasonable.

It was often twenty minutes too early.

Her partner would answer with a blank look, shame would rise, Carys would interpret the blankness as indifference, and the second argument would begin before the first nervous-system event had ended.

What changed their relationship was not a better apology script.

It was learning that recovery and repair are different stages.

Fictional composite case.

The Four-Stage Repair Cycle

The cycle is:

> **Recover → Reconnect → Review → Revise.**

Each stage has a different purpose.

Problems occur when couples skip a stage or attempt several at once.

Recover

Restore enough physical and cognitive capacity for ordinary functioning.

Reconnect

Give a small signal that the relationship still exists and the conflict is not the whole world.

Review

Discuss what happened, including impact and responsibility.

Revise

Change the plan so the same information is not wasted.

This is not a rigid timetable. A mild shutdown may move through all four stages in an evening. A severe mixed episode may require sleep before review. The sequence matters more than the clock.

Stage One: Recover

Recovery is physical before it is philosophical.

After intense overload, the body may need quiet, darkness, food, hydration, sleep, repetitive movement, a shower, medication taken as normally prescribed, or reduced social contact. After trauma activation, the person may need time for arousal to settle and orientation to become stable.

The supporting partner may also need recovery.

You might be shaking.

Your heart may be racing.

You may be angry.

You may feel desperate to know whether the relationship is okay.

You may want an apology before you can sleep.

Those needs matter. They do not automatically determine the timing.

If both people are depleted, separate recovery may be the best first step.

Signs You Are Still in Recovery

Do not rely only on whether the person has stopped crying or shouting.

Capacity may still be low if:

- speech remains slow or minimal;
- the person cannot tolerate ordinary light or sound;
- simple decisions remain hard;

- the body is still shaking or highly tense;
- questions produce immediate distress;
- the person appears exhausted or confused;
- either partner is still rehearsing accusations rather than listening;
- the supporting partner feels an urgent need to "get closure now."

Urgency is often a sign that you are not ready for review.

Stage Two: Reconnect

Reconnection is not the same as resolution.

It may be one sentence:

"I love you. We can talk tomorrow."

Or:

"We are both safe. I am going to bed in the other room. Goodnight."

Or:

"I am still upset, and I am not leaving the relationship."

Or a practical gesture agreed in advance: tea left outside the door, a texted heart, feeding the dog, sitting at the other end of the sofa.

The purpose is to interrupt all-or-nothing thinking.

A conflict can remain unresolved without the relationship being erased.

For trauma survivors who fear abandonment, this signal may be especially regulating. For autistic partners who fear renewed verbal demand, the signal must be brief enough that it does not secretly reopen the discussion.

Reconnection Must Be Honest

Do not use false reassurance.

If the episode involved serious harm, you do not need to say, "Everything is fine."

You can say:

"We are safe. I am not discussing this tonight. We will decide what happens next tomorrow."

Connection does not require pretending there is no consequence.

Stage Three: Review

Review is the first stage in which the relationship story becomes central again.

Use facts before interpretations.

A useful five-question review is:

25. **What was happening before the episode?**
26. **What did each of us notice as capacity changed?**
27. **What helped?**
28. **What made it worse?**
29. **What harm or unresolved issue still needs repair?**

Then ask a sixth:

30. **What will we change next time?**

This keeps the review from becoming a blame ceremony.

Separate Cause, Impact, and Responsibility

These three ideas are often tangled.

Cause

"I was overloaded after work and the noise pushed me past capacity."

Impact

"You shouted while I was holding the baby, and I became frightened."

Responsibility

"I need to leave the kitchen earlier when I reach amber, and I need to apologise for frightening you."

Notice what this structure avoids.

The cause does not deny impact.

The impact does not require claiming malicious intent.

Responsibility is specific enough to change behaviour.

Intention Is Not the Only Measure

Many couples get stuck in an intention-impact loop.

“I didn't mean it that way.”

“But it hurt.”

“I said I didn't mean it.”

“I know, but it still hurt.”

Intent matters morally. Impact matters relationally.

A mature repair can contain both:

“I did not intend to threaten you. I understand that standing in the doorway while shouting made you feel trapped. I will not stand in doorways during conflict again.”

This is stronger than either self-condemnation or defensiveness.

Do Not Use Shame as a Substitute for Repair

After dysregulation, autistic people and trauma survivors may experience intense shame. Shame can sound like accountability because it is painful.

“I am horrible.”

“You should leave me.”

“I ruin everything.”

“I don't deserve you.”

These statements may be sincere. They can also derail repair by requiring the hurt partner to reassure the person who caused harm.

Try redirecting:

“I am not asking whether you are a bad person. I am asking what happened and what needs to change.”

Specificity is kinder than global condemnation because it creates a path forward.

The Supporting Partner Also Repairs

Do not assume the autistic trauma survivor is always the person who caused the rupture.

The supporting partner may have:

- followed someone who was asking for space;
- blocked an exit while trying to continue a conversation;
- mocked sensory needs;
- demanded eye contact;
- used diagnostic language as an insult;
- touched without consent;
- shouted;
- threatened breakup to obtain reassurance;
- dismissed real trauma as "just a trigger";
- forced disclosure;
- continued an argument after the other person had clearly lost capacity.

Repair is mutual where responsibility is mutual.

The double empathy literature is useful here because it challenges the assumption that mixed-neurotype communication failure sits entirely inside the autistic person. Misunderstanding can be reciprocal (Jones et al., 2024).

Stage Four: Revise

A review without revision becomes archaeology.

You keep discovering what went wrong and then rebuilding the same conditions.

Revision asks:

What do we change in the environment?

What do we change in timing?

What do we change in communication?

What does each person need to practise?

What requires professional help?

Examples:

- difficult conversations move from bedtime to late morning;
- the autistic partner uses an amber signal earlier;
- the supporting partner stops following during shutdown;
- the couple adds a written return time;
- headphones are kept in the car;
- trauma therapy resumes;
- alcohol is removed from conflict situations;
- one partner begins individual therapy for abandonment panic;
- financial discussions use a printed agenda;
- children go to a predetermined room during adult dysregulation;
- objects that are commonly thrown are moved out of the conflict area while a larger safety plan is developed.

Revision turns compassion into engineering.

When the Same Repair Fails Repeatedly

If the same incident occurs again and again, do not keep calling the same apology progress.

Repeated harm requires increasing intervention.

That may mean:

- more serious environmental change;
- formal couples therapy with an autism- and trauma-informed clinician;
- individual trauma treatment;
- occupational therapy or sensory assessment;
- medication review with a prescriber when relevant;
- temporary separation of living spaces;
- financial safeguards;
- a domestic abuse service if coercion or violence is present;
- reconsidering whether the relationship is sustainable.

A repair cycle is not a promise that every relationship should continue.

It is a method for discovering whether the relationship can learn.

The Debrief Sheet

Use one page.

Event: ________

Baseline load: ________

Early signs: ________

Likely state: meltdown / shutdown / flashback / mixed / unknown

What helped: ________

What worsened it: ________

Impact on me: ________

Impact on you: ________

What needs apology or repair: ________

What issue remains unresolved: ________

One change for next time: ________

Do not turn this into paperwork after every difficult emotion. Use it for episodes important enough to teach you something.

The Point of Repair

Repair is not proving that love survived.

It is showing that the relationship can learn from pain.

Recovery restores capacity.

Reconnection restores a thread.

Review restores reality.

Revision protects the future.

When all four happen, the episode becomes information rather than destiny.

Repair Language That Does Not Collapse Into Blame

Couples often need sentence structures because the emotional stakes make improvisation difficult. Try these.

To name impact without guessing intent

"When you ___, I experienced ___."

"When you shouted from the doorway, I felt trapped and frightened."

To explain state without erasing impact

"I was in severe overload. That explains why my capacity collapsed. It does not change the fact that I frightened you."

To request a future change

"Next time I need you to ___."

"Next time you notice speech dropping, I need you to stop asking questions and use the card."

To take responsibility without global shame

"I am responsible for ___. My prevention step is ___."

To preserve an unresolved issue

"We are repaired enough to stop for tonight. The original issue is still open, and we will return to it on ___."

These are not scripts to recite mechanically. They are ways of keeping cause, impact, responsibility, and future action in separate lanes.

A strong apology should usually become more specific over time, not more dramatic. "I am sorry for everything" may feel intense but tells the couple little. "I am sorry I followed you after you used the shutdown signal; next time I will send one check-in text and wait" creates behavioural evidence of learning.

Repair After Words That Cannot Be Taken Back

Verbal harm creates a special problem because overload may explain why inhibition failed, but the words still enter the relationship. "I hate you," "You're useless," or a cruel reference to someone's trauma may continue echoing long after the nervous system settles.

Do not demand that the hurt partner immediately accept, "I didn't mean it." Meaning matters, but memory does not disappear on command.

A fuller repair includes:

31. Name the exact words.
32. State whether they reflect a belief you actually hold.
33. Acknowledge the impact.
34. Identify the condition that made verbal control fail.
35. Change the prevention plan.
36. Accept that trust may recover more slowly than your shame.

For example:

"I said you were pathetic. I do not believe that. I said it while overwhelmed and trying to make the conversation stop. It was cruel and it hit a place I know is painful for you. Next time I reach that level, my responsibility is to leave the conversation before I start attacking. I understand you may not feel fine just because I have apologised."

This is accountability without pretending the episode occurred in a vacuum.

Chapter 11: Talking When Nobody Is in Crisis

"Can we talk?"

Wren Hollis looked up from her laptop.

"About what?"

"Us."

Wren's shoulders tightened.

"That is not a topic."

Her partner, Arden Blythe, laughed once—not because it was funny, but because he had never heard their communication problem stated so precisely.

He had meant the sentence as intimacy.

Wren had heard an undefined task with no scope, no duration, no preparation time, and a high probability of criticism.

Fictional composite case.

The best crisis protocol cannot compensate for poor communication the rest of the week.

The calmer hours are where couples build the conditions that make dysregulation less likely and repair more reliable.

Stop Treating Spontaneous Speech as the Highest Form of Intimacy

Many relationship cultures prize the ability to "just talk."

Sit down.

Open up.

Say how you feel.

Respond immediately.

Maintain eye contact.

Read tone.

Infer what is meant.

Stay emotionally available until the issue is resolved.

That format can be demanding for anyone. For some autistic adults, it combines several difficult tasks at once.

The solution is not to abandon emotional intimacy.

It is to separate intimacy from one preferred communication performance.

The Double Empathy Problem in the Living Room

The double empathy problem proposes that misunderstanding between autistic and non-autistic people can be reciprocal rather than evidence of a one-sided autistic lack of empathy. Research has found that interaction quality and interpretation can differ depending on neurotype pairing and that non-autistic observers also contribute to misreading autistic people (Jones et al., 2024).

This is useful in relationships because it moves the question from:

“What is wrong with the autistic partner's communication?”

to:

“What does this pair need in order to understand each other?”

That shift does not mean every communication style works equally well in every situation. Directness can still hurt. Indirectness can still confuse. Silence can still frighten. Repetition can still exhaust.

It means repair is a translation problem both people participate in.

Make the Topic Finite

Compare:

“We need to talk about our relationship.”

with:

“I want twenty minutes tomorrow to decide how we handle Sunday visits with my parents.”

The second has boundaries.

It tells the nervous system:

- what the topic is;
- when it begins;
- roughly how long it lasts;
- what decision is expected.

Predictability does not remove emotion. It reduces unnecessary uncertainty around emotion.

One Topic at a Time

Relationship conflicts often become bundles.

“We're talking about money, but this is exactly what happened with Christmas, and you never apologised for the holiday, and your mother does the same thing, and we haven't had sex in three weeks.”

The bundle may feel emotionally coherent to the speaker. It is cognitively expensive.

Try a parking list.

Current topic: credit-card balance.

Parked: Christmas, mother, sex.

The parked items are not dismissed. They are protected from being lost inside overload.

Send the Agenda First

Written preparation can reduce the feeling of ambush.

An agenda might say:

Saturday relationship meeting - 11:00-11:30

37. Confirm next month's childcare schedule.
38. Discuss one concern about spending.
39. Decide whether to book couples therapy.

No other topics unless both agree.

This may look formal for a marriage.

So is a shared calendar, a mortgage, a school timetable, or a medication schedule.

Structure is not the opposite of love. For many couples, structure makes tenderness possible because fewer cognitive resources are spent on uncertainty.

Processing Time Is Not Evasion by Definition

Some people formulate their best response after the conversation.

They need time to identify feelings, organise language, or understand what a question means.

Alexithymia—the difficulty identifying and describing emotions—is common among autistic people but not universal. A systematic review and meta-analysis found higher alexithymia in autistic groups while emphasising that it should not be treated as synonymous with autism (Kinnaird et al., 2019).

That distinction matters. Do not assume your partner "doesn't know their feelings" because they are autistic.

But if emotional identification is difficult for them, questions such as "How do you feel about our marriage?" may be genuinely hard to answer on demand.

Try narrower prompts:

"Do you want more or less time together on weeknights?"

"When I cancelled the plan, did you feel more disappointed, angry, frightened, or something else?"

"Would you rather answer tomorrow?"

Written Communication Can Carry Serious Emotion

A common fear is that text makes conflict cold.

It can. It can also make conflict safer.

Writing allows:

- slower processing;
- fewer interruptions;
- exact wording;
- rereading;
- time to regulate before responding;
- less eye-contact demand;
- a record of agreements.

It can also become harmful if used for enormous midnight essays, hostile message barrages, or avoidance of any real-time contact.

Use rules.

For example:

- maximum 500 words per person per round;
- no more than one response before a break;
- no messaging during work unless urgent;
- factual decisions summarised at the end;
- emotional topics can move to voice or therapy if text becomes harsher than intended.

A medium is a tool. Design how you use it.

Literal Versus Implied Meaning

Mixed-neurotype couples often suffer from invisible expectations.

"Fine" may mean "I am angry and want you to notice."

To a more literal partner, it may mean "fine."

"You can go if you want" may function as a test of loyalty.

To a literal partner, it may be permission.

"I shouldn't have to ask" may feel self-evident to one person and impossible to the other.

This does not mean the autistic partner can never infer. It means the couple should not build important relationship outcomes around tests whose rules are hidden.

Say the need.

"I want you to stay."

"I need reassurance."

"I am angry even though I said fine."

"I want you to notice chores without me assigning them, so we need a system for shared ownership."

Directness reduces the number of relationship problems disguised as mind-reading exams.

Eye Contact Is Not a Truth Detector

Do not require eye contact during serious conversations as evidence of attention, remorse, or honesty.

Some autistic people listen better when looking away, moving, drawing, or focusing on an object. Eye contact itself can consume attention or feel intense.

Instead, check understanding directly:

"Can you tell me what you heard me ask?"

That is more useful than "Look at me."

Build a Pause That Does Not Feel Like Abandonment

Every couple in this book needs a pause protocol.

A good pause contains:

Reason: "I am losing capacity."

Duration: "I need forty minutes."

Relationship signal: "I am not leaving the relationship."

Return: "I will come back at nine."

The person requesting a pause has a responsibility to return or update.

The person waiting has a responsibility not to pursue unless safety requires it.

This is the communication version of the Shutdown Protocol.

Use the Twenty-Minute Low-Load Meeting

Try this format once a week.

Minute 0-2: Bandwidth check

Each person gives a number from 0 to 10.

If either is below the agreed threshold, reschedule.

Minute 2-5: One good thing

Not forced gratitude. One concrete thing that worked.

Minute 5-15: One issue

Use an agenda sent earlier.

Minute 15-18: Decision or next step

What happens next? Who owns it? By when?

Minute 18-20: Close

Confirm any unresolved issue and the next meeting.

The meeting ends on time unless both actively agree to continue.

Predictable ending is part of safety.

Do Not Turn Every Interaction Into Therapy

If a couple learns psychological language, ordinary life can become clinical.

“Your tone triggered my nervous system.”

“You're masking.”

“That's your attachment wound.”

“You're dysregulated.”

“That's alexithymia.”

Sometimes the most accurate sentence is simpler:

“That hurt.”

“I disagree.”

“I need quiet.”

“I forgot.”

“I don't want to go.”

Psychological language should clarify life, not replace it.

The Communication Standard

A communication system is working when both people can:

- raise necessary subjects;
- understand what is being asked;
- pause without disappearing;
- disagree without diagnosing each other;
- use more than one communication medium;
- return after overload;
- state needs directly;
- repair misunderstandings;
- keep safety intact.

You do not need to become a perfectly articulate couple.

You need a system that still works when the topic matters.

Five Conversations Worth Redesigning

Some subjects carry so much sensory, emotional, or trauma load that they deserve their own format rather than being handled whenever they arise.

Money

Use documents. Separate facts from accusation. Share balances and numbers before discussing meaning. Decide what requires an immediate decision and what does not.

Sex

Do not conduct the entire sexual relationship through moments of initiation and rejection. Talk outside the bedroom about touch, desire, sensory needs, trauma reminders, and how each person wants a no to be handled.

Family and in-laws

Make expectations explicit: arrival time, departure time, transport, recovery, what information may be shared about diagnoses, and who handles conflict with relatives.

Chores

Avoid the parent-child dynamic of one person assigning every task. Create ownership. A task belongs to someone from noticing through completion, even if the method is adapted.

Parenting

Do not wait until both adults are overwhelmed to decide who takes over. Create contingency rules for red-zone periods and a later method for balancing the load.

The point is not to make marriage bureaucratic. It is to stop repeatedly placing the highest-stakes subjects inside the least supportive conditions.

When a topic reliably causes dysregulation, redesign the container before blaming the content.

Empathy Without Mind-Reading

Partners sometimes reach a painful conclusion: "If they loved me, they would know." The autistic partner may reach the mirror conclusion: "If you loved me, you would say what you mean."

Both are asking for recognition. They are asking through different communication rules.

Replace tests with explicit bridges.

Instead of waiting to see whether your partner notices you are upset, say, "I am upset and I want comfort."

Instead of assuming a direct statement has no emotional layer, ask, “Do you want me to solve this, listen, or reassure you?”

Instead of interpreting flat affect as lack of concern, ask for the person's understanding of what happened.

Instead of using a partner's difficulty reading you as proof of low empathy, look at how they respond once the need is clear.

Empathy in a relationship is not only spontaneous inference. It is also willingness to learn another person's signals and act with care after receiving clear information.

The supporting partner should not have to narrate every emotional need forever. Shared learning should make recognition easier over time. But making important needs explicit is not a lesser form of intimacy. It is often the route through which mixed-neurotype intimacy becomes dependable.

Chapter 12: Reduce the Load, Not the Person

Thirty-eight minutes.

That was how long it took Sloane Everly to sit in the parked car after work before she could enter her own house without feeling that every sound inside would cut through her.

Her partner used to interpret those thirty-eight minutes as rejection.

Later, they treated them as a medicalised ritual that could never be interrupted.

Both interpretations were too simple.

The better question was: what function did the time serve, and how could the household make room for that function without making one adult disappear from family life?

Fictional composite case; the number is illustrative, not a research finding.

Accommodation Should Increase Life, Not Shrink It

The word accommodation can sound like special treatment. In reality, every relationship contains accommodations.

One partner sleeps with a fan.

One needs coffee before conversation.

One hates driving at night.

One needs advance notice before guests.

One works best in silence.

Autism may make some needs more pronounced and less optional. Trauma may add conditions under which safety and predictability matter intensely.

The question is not whether to accommodate.

The question is **what the accommodation accomplishes and who pays for it.**

Start With Function

Sloane's thirty-eight minutes in the car provide sensory and social decompression after a customer-facing job.

If the function is recovery, alternatives might include:

- a quiet room inside the house;
- a shorter decompression routine plus headphones;
- a job adjustment that reduces end-of-day overload;
- changing who handles the noisiest household task at that time;
- moving family connection to later in the evening.

If the family simply declares "Sloane cannot be approached after work," the accommodation may become rigid and shift every burden to the other partner.

Functional thinking gives more options.

Autistic Burnout Changes the Baseline

Burnout is not just a bad day.

In the qualitative study that helped define autistic burnout in the research literature, autistic adults described chronic exhaustion, reduced access to skills, and lower tolerance to stimulus, often in the context of prolonged demands and inadequate relief (Raymaker et al., 2020).

During burnout, the threshold for meltdown or shutdown may be much lower than usual. Skills that were previously reliable may become less accessible. Social contact may cost more. Sensory input may become harder to tolerate.

Partners sometimes react by saying:

"But you used to be able to do this."

That observation may be true.

It does not prove current capacity.

At the same time, burnout should not become a permanent explanation for a household arrangement in which one partner carries everything indefinitely. Severe or prolonged functional decline deserves clinical attention and practical support.

Conduct a Household Load Audit

Walk through a normal week.

Where does demand cluster?

Morning

Alarms, light, dressing, children, breakfast texture, time pressure, commuting, decision-making.

Workday

Masking, meetings, sensory environment, unpredictable requests, travel, social contact.

Transition home

Traffic, shops, childcare pickup, sudden change from work role to family role.

Evening

Noise, cooking smells, multiple conversations, homework, chores, relationship decisions, touch, television, planning tomorrow.

Night

Sleep difficulty, nightmares, different temperature needs, snoring, trauma-related hypervigilance, delayed processing of the day's events.

Then ask:

What can be simplified?

What can be automated?

What can be moved?

What can be made more predictable?

What is being done because "normal couples do it this way" rather than because it works?

Reduce Hidden Decisions

Decision load is easy to overlook.

"What do you want for dinner?"

"Where should we go?"

"When do you want to talk?"

"Which bill should we pay first?"

"What do you want to do this weekend?"

Choice can be liberating. Endless open choice can be exhausting.

Use defaults.

Tuesday dinner is one of three meals.

Relationship meetings happen Saturday morning unless moved.

The quiet room has a standard setup.

Visitors require notice.

The couple has a default plan for cancelled events.

Defaults preserve capacity for decisions that matter more.

Reduce Sensory Conflict Without Creating One Person's House

A shared home contains competing sensory needs.

One partner needs silence. The other regulates through music.

One wants low light. The other becomes depressed in dark rooms.

One dislikes touch. The other experiences touch as central to connection.

One needs a cold bedroom. The other cannot sleep cold.

There may be no single perfect environment.

Use zones and times.

Headphones rather than silence for everyone.

Task lighting rather than darkening the entire house.

Separate blankets.

A quiet room and a lively room.

Scheduled touch rather than either constant touch or none.

The goal is not to make the non-autistic partner live in an autism clinic. It is to design a home where both bodies can exist.

Predictability Is Not the Same as Control

Trauma and autism can both increase the value of predictability for different reasons.

Predictability can reduce switching demands, decision load, and threat uncertainty.

But a relationship cannot eliminate surprise.

Children get sick.

Flights are cancelled.

Jobs change.

People change their minds.

The target is **supported flexibility**, not total control.

A useful change protocol is:

40. Say what changed.
41. Say what has not changed.
42. Give the new plan.
43. Allow processing time where possible.
44. Reduce optional demands around the change.

Example:

"The restaurant cancelled our booking. We are still having dinner together. We can choose takeaway or the quiet café. We don't have to decide for ten minutes."

That is predictability inside change.

Trauma Triggers: Remove Danger, Not All Discomfort

If a particular situation is genuinely unsafe, remove it.

If it is a trauma reminder but currently safe, the long-term clinical goal may not be permanent avoidance. Evidence-based PTSD therapies often work directly with trauma memories, beliefs, and avoided safe situations under professional guidance (VA, n.d.-b; NICE, 2018).

A partner should not force exposure.

You also should not redesign the entire family around avoiding every reminder forever.

This is where collaboration with a trauma therapist matters. Ask:

"What accommodation supports functioning now?"

"What avoidance is part of the clinical problem?"

"What should the partner do, and what should be left to therapy?"

The answers will vary.

Household Labour Is Part of Regulation

A common hidden problem is that one partner becomes protected from overload by transferring tasks to the other partner.

Phone calls are stressful, so the spouse makes every call.

Shopping is sensory, so the spouse shops.

Children are noisy, so the spouse handles bedtime.

Paperwork is overwhelming, so the spouse manages finances.

Family events are difficult, so the spouse attends alone and manages explanations.

One accommodation at a time may make sense.

Together they can create an unequal adult life.

The question becomes:

If this task is inaccessible in its current form, how else can responsibility be carried?

Online shopping.

Email instead of phone.

Noise protection during bedtime.

A financial app.

Paid help if affordable.

Task exchange: one partner does forms while the other handles laundry.

Shared responsibility does not require identical tasks.

It requires an arrangement neither person experiences as exploitation.

The Difference Between Recovery Time and Exemption

Recovery time has a beginning and an end.

It serves a function.

It improves later capacity.

Exemption is indefinite and transfers the cost to someone else without review.

If Sloane needs thirty-eight minutes after work and then participates in dinner, that may be a workable recovery accommodation.

If "I need to decompress" means Sloane is unavailable every evening while her partner cooks, parents, cleans, and manages tomorrow, the system needs revision.

The issue is not whether Sloane's overload is real.

The issue is whether the household has solved overload by creating another person's burnout.

The Household Load Audit Exercise

Create four columns:

High-cost tasks

What repeatedly pushes either partner toward overload or trauma activation?

Function

What makes the task costly: sensory, social, cognitive, physical, emotional, trauma-related?

Redesign

How can the task be changed without simply handing it to the other person?

Ownership

Who is responsible for the redesigned task?

Then review monthly during unstable periods.

A good home is not one in which nobody is ever uncomfortable.

It is one in which predictable, unnecessary load is not mistaken for virtue.

The Rule to Keep

Reduce the load.

Do not reduce the person.

An autistic partner should not have to erase their sensory reality to be lovable.

A trauma survivor should not have to pretend reminders do not exist.

The supporting partner should not have to become smaller so everyone else can remain regulated.

The household is the thing you redesign.

When Work Is the Hidden Third Partner

Many couples focus on evening behaviour without examining what employment requires during the day. A job that demands constant masking, unpredictable social interaction, painful sensory exposure, or rapid switching can consume most available capacity before the relationship receives any.

This does not mean the working autistic partner should quit impulsively or that the other partner must accept permanent evening unavailability. It means work belongs in the systems analysis.

Questions to consider include:

- Which parts of the workday are most costly?
- Are accommodations available through the employer or local disability framework?
- Could commuting, hours, workspace, communication format, or task allocation change?
- Is a different role financially realistic?
- Does the household schedule assume the person has full capacity immediately after work?
- Is the supporting partner also overloaded by paid work and then carrying the second shift at home?

A relationship can become resentful when one person's paid work is treated as legitimate exhaustion and the other person's domestic labour is treated as infinitely flexible. Put both on the page.

The integrated model asks where capacity is being spent across the whole system. Sometimes the most effective "relationship intervention" is a workplace adjustment, a childcare change, paid cleaning, or a different commute.

Fair Does Not Always Mean Equal

Couples can become trapped by the idea that fairness requires identical tasks. It does not.

If one partner finds phone calls intensely difficult but can manage detailed online administration, task exchange may be fairer than equal call-taking. If one partner cannot tolerate the supermarket but can cook reliably, online ordering plus cooking may create balanced ownership.

The danger is using disability language to turn unequal contribution into a permanent fact that cannot be discussed. Fairness requires looking at the total system:

- time spent;
- cognitive effort;

- sensory cost;
- emotional labour;
- financial contribution;
- childcare;
- invisible planning;
- recovery needs.

Do not compare only visible chores. The partner who makes every appointment, anticipates every crisis, remembers every school form, and manages every family relationship may be carrying a large invisible load.

A fair system can be asymmetrical. It cannot be unquestionable. Review it when one person becomes resentful, ill, burned out, unemployed, pregnant, newly employed, or otherwise changed.

The goal is not 50/50 on every Tuesday. It is a durable sense that both adults are carrying the shared life in ways that reflect their actual capacity.

Part IV: Staying Connected Without Losing Yourself

Chapter 13: Stop Becoming the Full-Time Regulator

Two mugs were on the table. One was still hot.

Pippa Sterling had made both, carried them into the sitting room, placed her partner's mug beside the usual chair, lowered the blinds, turned off the television, checked whether the neighbour's dog was barking, moved a pile of mail out of sight, and postponed the question she had planned to ask about rent.

Her partner had not yet come home.

Pippa was already regulating the evening for two people.

Fictional composite case.

Care can become a job so gradually that the person doing it does not notice when the relationship changes shape.

You begin by being considerate.

You end by managing another adult's nervous system before they enter the room.

Caregiver Burden Is Real

PTSD affects more than the person diagnosed. The VA's National Center for PTSD notes that partners and family members can experience caregiver burden, stress, frustration, fatigue, and their own psychological distress as symptoms affect family life (VA, n.d.-d).

Autism can create different but overlapping support demands, especially when the autistic adult is in burnout, has high support needs, or has gone decades without adequate accommodations.

When autism and CPTSD coexist, the partner may begin carrying several roles:

- spouse;
- translator;
- appointment coordinator;

- sensory planner;
- trigger monitor;
- conflict de-escalator;
- executive-function support;
- therapist substitute;
- family spokesperson;
- crisis responder;
- income stabiliser;
- parent to children;
- and, quietly, parent to the partner.

That last shift is dangerous to intimacy.

You Cannot Be a Spouse and a Nervous System

You can help regulate.

Humans co-regulate naturally. A calm voice, familiar presence, predictable routine, or supportive touch can reduce distress.

But co-regulation is not the same as becoming the only condition under which another adult can function.

If your partner cannot attend an appointment unless you organise it, cannot recover from conflict unless you say exactly the right words, cannot manage any trauma reminder without you, and cannot tolerate your independent needs because your independence feels threatening, the relationship has become structurally fragile.

You are not required to become indispensable.

In fact, a healthy support system usually aims in the opposite direction: more options, more skills, more professional support, more self-knowledge, more ways to recover—not one exhausted spouse holding the entire structure up.

Hypervigilance Can Transfer

The supporting partner may begin living in anticipatory mode.

You notice the refrigerator hum before your partner does.

You scan the restaurant for exits.

You monitor how much they slept.

You read their face when a family member makes a comment.

You decide whether the children can have friends over based on your partner's mood.

You do not mention your bad day because theirs looks worse.

You choose your words so carefully that speaking becomes work.

You may call this empathy.

Some of it is empathy.

Some may be hypervigilance.

The difference is how much freedom remains in your own body and life.

The Mine/Yours/Ours Circles

Draw three circles.

Mine

Your responsibilities include:

- your own safety;
- your communication choices;
- your boundaries;
- your therapy or support if needed;
- your friendships;
- your sleep and health;
- your financial decisions within agreed boundaries;
- your behaviour during conflict;
- deciding what you will and will not remain in.

Yours

Your partner's responsibilities include:

- learning their own warning signs where possible;
- communicating preferred support when calm;
- using professional care where needed;
- respecting your physical and emotional boundaries;

- returning to unfinished conversations;
- repairing harm they caused;
- carrying an adult share of life in a form compatible with their capacity;
- telling the truth about what they can and cannot do.

Ours

Shared responsibilities include:

- designing communication systems;
- making household agreements;
- parenting decisions;
- financial planning;
- sexual consent and intimacy agreements;
- adapting the environment;
- updating the Moment Map;
- deciding when couples support is needed;
- creating rituals of connection.

When "yours" moves steadily into "mine," resentment grows.

Partner Accommodation and Avoidance

PTSD research uses the term **partner accommodation** for ways loved ones alter their own behaviour in response to PTSD symptoms. Accommodation can be caring and useful, but research has also examined how some forms may reinforce avoidance or become associated with worse symptom patterns (VA, n.d.-c).

This idea should be applied carefully to autism because autistic accommodations are not the same as trauma avoidance. Reducing sensory harm, accepting alternative communication, or allowing needed recovery is not something to eliminate in pursuit of normality.

The integrated question is:

> **Is this adaptation helping the person live more fully, or is it making the whole household smaller?**

For example:

Noise-cancelling headphones at a wedding may increase participation.

Never attending any family event because distress is possible may reduce life.

Using text for difficult discussions may increase communication.

Refusing all discussion in every medium may reduce accountability.

Taking thirty minutes after work may increase family capacity later.

Being unavailable every evening may shift the entire household onto the other partner.

Function matters.

Resentment Is Information

Partners often feel ashamed of resentment because the person they love has genuine disabilities or trauma.

Resentment is not always morally accurate, but it often contains information.

Ask what it is pointing toward.

Unequal labour?

No appreciation?

Too little sleep?

No sexual or affectionate connection?

Constant fear?

No room for your emotions?

Promises that are never revised even when they repeatedly fail?

A life organised around crisis?

Loss of friends?

Financial dependence?

No privacy?

Do not immediately convert resentment into accusation.

Translate it into a need or system problem.

"I resent doing everything" becomes "We need an explicit division of labour that accounts for capacity without making me responsible for all inaccessible tasks."

"I resent your shutdowns" becomes "I need a reliable return signal so I am not left in uncertainty for days."

"I resent your trauma" may become "I have become the only person you use for crisis support, and I cannot sustain that role."

Translated resentment can be worked with.

Keep Parts of Your Life Untouched by the Diagnosis

You need experiences in which you are not monitoring, adapting, interpreting, or helping.

Friendships.

Work.

Reading.

Sport.

Faith.

Art.

Time alone.

Time with family.

A room, desk, walk, class, or routine that belongs to you.

This is not selfish separation. It is identity maintenance.

The relationship should be one part of a life, even when it is a central part.

If every independent activity triggers crisis, guilt, punishment, or accusation, professional support is needed. A partner's trauma fear does not create ownership over your time.

Build a Wider Support Network

Ask a difficult question:

If I became ill for two weeks, what would happen?

Could your partner contact their therapist?

Could they order food?

Could they ask a friend for help?

Do they know their medications and appointments?

Can they use their grounding plan without you?

Can someone else support the children?

Could bills still be paid?

Resilience means the relationship can survive your temporary unavailability.

If the answer is no, the couple needs redundancy.

Professional support, family, friends, peer groups, practical services, written plans, automated systems, and independent skills all reduce pressure on the romantic bond.

The Partner's Own Therapy

Individual therapy for the supporting partner is not an admission that you are the problem.

It can give you a place to examine:

- why silence activates you;
- why you rescue;
- why boundaries feel cruel;
- whether you are living with abuse;
- how your own neurodivergence affects the relationship;
- grief about the partnership you expected;
- resentment;
- sexual disconnection;
- whether you want to stay.

The autistic trauma survivor should not be the only person in the relationship allowed a complicated inner life.

Stop Measuring Love by Endurance

One of the most harmful relationship myths is that staying proves love.

Sometimes staying is loving.

Sometimes leaving is necessary.

Sometimes temporary separation creates safety and treatment space.

Sometimes a relationship is incompatible even though both people are good.

Sometimes trauma and autism explain the suffering but do not make the partnership sustainable.

This book cannot decide that for you.

It can give you a clearer basis for deciding.

Ask:

Is there safety?

Is there mutual responsibility?

Can necessary subjects be discussed eventually?

Does repair happen?

Are plans updated?

Is treatment sought when needed?

Are both people allowed needs?

Is there affection, companionship, humour, sexuality if desired, shared purpose, or pleasure—not only management?

Do you still exist inside your own life?

These questions matter more than whether you have become exceptionally skilled at preventing meltdowns.

Pippa's Two Mugs

Pippa eventually noticed that her evening routine had become an attempt to guarantee her partner's regulation.

She did not stop being considerate.

She changed ownership.

Her partner chose the lighting setup and kept their own headphones by the door. They agreed that the first twenty minutes after work would be quiet. Pippa stopped scanning the house for every possible irritation. If the neighbour's dog barked, her partner handled their own headphones. If Pippa needed to raise a practical issue, she used the agreed meeting time rather than postponing indefinitely.

The mug remained.

The surveillance did not.

That is the goal: care without disappearance.

The Rescue Reflex

Some partners are drawn to rescue before they meet an autistic trauma survivor. They may have grown up keeping peace in an unpredictable family, caring for a parent, or learning that love means anticipating needs before they are spoken. A relationship with real support needs can make that pattern look especially virtuous.

Ask yourself:

- Do I feel needed only when I am solving something?
- Do I step in before my partner asks?
- Do I secretly believe things will collapse if I stop managing them?
- Do I resent tasks I volunteered to take over?
- Do I prevent natural consequences because I cannot tolerate my partner's distress?
- Do boundaries feel like cruelty?

If the answer is often yes, your work may involve tolerating another adult's discomfort without rushing to remove it.

This is different from refusing reasonable disability support. The distinction lies in ownership and consent. Support says, "Tell me which part you want help with." Rescue says, "I have already taken over because I do not believe you can handle the consequences."

A relationship becomes more adult when help can be requested, negotiated, refused, and revised.

The supporting partner's freedom is not a threat to the autistic trauma survivor's safety. In a stable relationship, each person's growing capacity should create more room for the other, not less.

Guilt When You Stop Overfunctioning

When you first stop doing tasks you have quietly absorbed, the relationship may feel worse before it feels better. Your partner may be genuinely distressed. You may see appointments missed, chores delayed, or discomfort rise. Guilt can send you back into rescue.

Change ownership gradually where safety allows.

Instead of suddenly refusing all help, say:

"I have been managing all your appointment reminders. I cannot continue doing that. I will help you set up a system this week, then the reminders will be yours."

Or:

"I will not make phone calls to your therapist for you. I can sit beside you while you send the email."

Support the transition without keeping permanent ownership.

There will be exceptions. During illness, acute trauma crisis, or severe burnout, partners often carry more. The issue is whether temporary support has a review point or silently becomes the new baseline.

Guilt is not always evidence that a boundary is wrong. Sometimes it is the feeling produced when you stop performing an old role.

Chapter 14: Building a Relationship Both Nervous Systems Can Live In

Arden Blythe and Carys Monroe stopped asking whether their marriage looked normal.

The question had cost them years.

Normal couples, they had believed, sleep in the same bed every night, attend most social events together, discuss problems face-to-face, enjoy spontaneous weekends, share the same friends, and know without asking when the other person wants comfort.

Their marriage did none of those things reliably.

Once they stopped grading themselves against an imagined couple, they could ask a better question:

> **Does the way we live allow both of us to be safe, responsible, connected, and recognisably ourselves?**

Fictional composite case.

This chapter moves beyond crisis management. A relationship cannot survive on excellent emergency protocols alone. The purpose of the Moment Map is to create enough stability that a life can be built around more than dysregulation.

Define Connection Together

One partner may experience connection through long conversation.

Another through parallel activity.

One through touch.

Another through shared projects.

One through spontaneous affection.

Another through predictable rituals.

One through frequent messaging.

Another through quiet presence.

Do not assume that different expressions mean different depth.

Ask directly:

"When do you feel most connected to me?"

"What kind of contact feels easy?"

"What kind feels effortful but worthwhile?"

"What do you miss?"

"What do you need less of?"

The answers may surprise you.

Create Predictable Connection Rituals

Trauma can make relationships feel uncertain. Autism can make spontaneity costly. Predictable connection can serve both without becoming mechanical.

Examples:

- tea together at 9 p.m.;
- a twenty-minute walk after dinner;
- Saturday morning breakfast outside the house;
- one shared television episode with phones away;
- a goodnight text even when sleeping separately;
- a weekly sexual or affectionate check-in without obligation to have sex;
- parallel reading in the same room;
- a shared hobby;
- ten quiet minutes after the children sleep.

Rituals reduce the amount of relationship maintenance that depends on guessing.

Intimacy Needs Its Own Sensory and Trauma Map

Sexual relationships can sit directly at the intersection of autism and trauma.

Touch may be sensory-seeking, sensory-aversive, context-dependent, or unpredictable under stress. Trauma may make certain positions, words, smells, types of restraint, lighting, nudity, or loss of control difficult.

Medication, depression, sleep, hormones, pain, and relationship resentment can also affect desire.

Do not turn every sexual problem into autism or trauma.

Do make consent explicit.

Useful conversations include:

- What kinds of touch are usually welcome?
- What changes when you are overloaded?
- Are there forms of touch that should never be used during conflict?
- How do we signal pause during sex?
- What words are triggering or confusing?
- Does advance planning increase safety or reduce desire?
- How do we handle a no without making it mean rejection of the relationship?

For trauma survivors, sexual difficulties may be appropriate to address with a trauma-informed clinician. For sensory barriers, an occupational therapist or autism-informed clinician may also help, depending on the need.

The partner is not a therapist. The bedroom should not become an exposure lab.

Separate Bedrooms Are a Tool, Not a Verdict

Sleep can be difficult for both autism and PTSD for many reasons. Noise, movement, temperature, nightmares, hypervigilance, touch sensitivity, different schedules, or insomnia may turn a shared bed into a nightly stressor.

Some couples sleep better separately and connect intentionally at other times.

Others deeply value shared sleep and make sensory adjustments.

There is no moral ranking.

A relationship is not measured by mattress geography.

The useful question is whether the arrangement supports rest and connection rather than avoidance or punishment.

Parenting Requires Explicit Contingency Plans

Children make spontaneity unavoidable.

The baby cries.

The school calls.

Plans change.

Noise is not optional.

A parent with autism and CPTSD may need clear contingency systems rather than an unrealistic promise that the environment will remain predictable.

Ask:

Who takes over if one parent reaches red?

How is that labour balanced later?

What happens if both are red?

Who are backup adults?

How do children learn that a parent's shutdown is not their fault?

How do you prevent children from becoming emotional caretakers?

What safety plan applies if adult dysregulation becomes frightening?

Parenting plans should protect the child and preserve the disabled parent's real role rather than either excluding them or pretending support needs do not exist.

Social Life Can Be Asymmetrical

You do not need identical social needs.

The non-autistic or differently neurodivergent partner may attend events alone.

The autistic partner may attend shorter periods with an exit plan.

The couple may host small gatherings rather than large ones.

One may have separate friendships.

The important question is whether asymmetry feels chosen and fair.

If one partner has become socially isolated because the other cannot tolerate them leaving, that is not simply a sensory accommodation.

If the autistic partner is forced into constant social performance to prove love, that is not fair either.

A sustainable relationship makes room for difference without using difference as ownership.

Choose Professional Help for the Actual Intersection

Many couples have encountered therapists who understand trauma but not autism, or autism but not trauma.

That mismatch can cause problems.

A therapist who understands trauma but not autism may interpret sensory avoidance as trauma avoidance, push eye contact or verbal emotional performance, or treat autistic traits as defences to be removed.

A therapist who understands autism but not trauma may normalise post-traumatic changes as autistic, miss re-experiencing, or underestimate the role of threat and relational history.

When looking for support, ask specific questions:

- How much experience do you have with autistic adults?
- How do you adapt sessions for sensory and communication needs?
- How do you assess trauma when symptoms overlap with autism?
- Which evidence-based PTSD treatments are you trained to provide?
- How do you distinguish accommodation from avoidance?
- How do you work with alexithymia or reduced speech without assuming either is universal?
- How do you include partners without making them responsible for treatment?
- How do you approach safety and possible abuse?

Evidence-based PTSD treatments include trauma-focused psychotherapies such as CPT, PE, and EMDR, while clinicians working with autistic people may need to adapt communication and delivery without discarding the treatment's active elements (VA, n.d.-b; Fisher et al., 2023).

Measure the Right Outcomes

If your measure of success is "no more meltdowns," you may miss progress.

If your measure is "my partner never gets triggered," you may reward avoidance.

If your measure is "we never fight," you may reward silence.

Better outcomes include:

- earlier recognition of overload;
- safer exits;
- fewer demands during shutdown;
- more reliable return to conversations;
- less frightening episodes;
- more personalised grounding;
- fewer preventable sensory collisions;
- stronger boundaries;
- more independent coping options;
- more honest division of labour;
- better repair;
- less partner hypervigilance;
- more shared pleasure;
- more room for separate identities.

These outcomes describe a relationship becoming more liveable, not a person becoming less autistic.

Write a Relationship Operating Agreement

This is not a legal contract. It is a shared description of how the relationship works best.

Include:

Communication

How do we raise difficult subjects?

How do we pause?

How do we return?

Dysregulation

Where are the five protocols kept?

What is our default mixed-state response?

Safety

What boundaries are absolute?

What situations require leaving or outside help?

Sensory life

What parts of the home are quiet, bright, social, or private?

Recovery

What time alone does each person need?

How is household labour handled during recovery?

Trauma

What grounding is welcome?

What belongs to professional treatment rather than partner support?

Intimacy

How is touch negotiated?

How do we handle a no?

Social life

What do we attend together, separately, or briefly?

Parenting or dependants

What is the backup plan?

Individual life

What time, friendships, hobbies, and spaces belong separately to each person?

Review

When do we update this agreement?

The agreement should change as capacity, treatment, work, parenting, health, and knowledge change.

A Relationship Can Be Unusual and Healthy

Perhaps you communicate serious issues by email.

Perhaps you sleep separately.

Perhaps you take two cars to family events so one person can leave early.

Perhaps you have a no-touch signal.

Perhaps one of you does all phone calls while the other handles all financial spreadsheets.

Perhaps you schedule sex because unpredictability creates anxiety.

Perhaps you spend evenings in parallel rather than in constant conversation.

None of these arrangements is a failure if both people understand them, consent to them, and remain able to raise their needs.

The aim is not normal.

The aim is mutual viability.

When Love Is Not Enough

It is possible to understand every chapter in this book and still decide the relationship cannot continue.

Maybe there is abuse.

Maybe one person refuses accountability.

Maybe needs are fundamentally incompatible.

Maybe one partner cannot tolerate the amount of caregiving required.

Maybe repeated trauma activation has made the relationship itself unsafe for one or both.

Maybe separation is the healthiest form of boundary available.

A good relationship book should not trap its reader inside the relationship.

The promise was never "stay at all costs."

The promise was to help you see more clearly, respond more safely, and remain a person while you love another person.

Sometimes that clarity strengthens commitment.

Sometimes it changes its form.

The Operating Test

Return to the question Arden and Carys finally asked:

> **Does the way we live allow both of us to be safe, responsible, connected, and recognisably ourselves?**

If the answer is increasingly yes, the relationship is learning.

If the answer is repeatedly no, the next step is not more endurance.

It is more truth.

What a Good Therapist Should Not Do

Knowing what to look for also means knowing what should concern you.

Be cautious if a clinician:

- treats every autistic trait as pathology to eliminate;
- assumes every request for predictability is trauma avoidance;
- tells the supporting partner to tolerate frightening behaviour without a safety plan;
- interprets all shutdown as manipulation without assessing capacity;
- interprets all relationship criticism as a trauma trigger rather than examining the content;
- pushes sensory or emotional exposure without informed consent and a clear clinical rationale;
- asks the partner to become a co-therapist outside an agreed treatment model;
- uses stereotypes about autistic empathy, intimacy, gender, or competence;

- dismisses domestic abuse concerns because the person causing harm is disabled or traumatised;
- promises that trauma treatment will make the person "less autistic."

A competent clinician should be able to tolerate two truths at once: disability may require adaptation, and adult relationships still require consent, safety, and responsibility.

Therapy should increase clarity and functioning. It should not merely provide more sophisticated language for the same stuck cycle.

What Long-Term Stability Actually Looks Like

Stable does not mean symptom-free. It means the relationship is less often surprised by its own patterns.

A stable couple may still have meltdowns. They know where each person goes and what language to use.

Shutdown may still occur. A return signal prevents days of uncertainty.

Trauma reminders may still arise. The survivor has professional treatment and personalised grounding rather than relying only on the spouse.

The supporting partner may still become activated. They recognise pursuit earlier and stop before it becomes another source of load.

Household plans still fail sometimes. They are revised without turning every failure into a verdict on love.

Most important, calm life becomes larger than crisis life. The couple talks about films, work, children, food, politics, travel, hobbies, sex, jokes, plans, boredom, and ordinary annoyances. The diagnosis is present without being the central topic every day.

That is an understated but meaningful measure of progress: the relationship contains enough safety that autism and trauma no longer need to explain every hour.

Conclusion: Love Without Self-Erasure

You will probably misread some moments.

That is not a pessimistic ending. It is the reason this method is built around response rather than certainty.

You may think a shutdown is trauma activation.

You may think a trauma response is overload.

Your partner may not know either.

A day of burnout may change every familiar sign. A real relationship conflict may sit beneath the dysregulation. Your own fear may alter what you see.

The goal is not to become infallible.

The goal is to become safer and more accurate than panic.

Return to the Five Assets

When you are unsure, return to the spine of the book.

The Moment Map

Is anyone unsafe? What was building? Where is capacity moving? What reduces pressure?

The Meltdown Protocol

Protect safety. Subtract input. Use fewer words. Stop debate. Keep touch consensual. Allow recovery. Return to accountability later.

The Shutdown Protocol

Stop demanding speech. Lower bandwidth. Reduce sensory load. Use a return signal. Resume the issue after capacity returns.

The Flashback Protocol

> **Stop the conflict. Make present safety concrete. Orient gently to now. Offer personalised grounding. Do not interrogate memory. Keep touch consensual.**

The Mixed/Unclear Protocol

> **Use the common denominator: safety, less sensory input, fewer words, one gentle present-time cue, no surprise touch, and a choice between space and quiet company. Name it later.**

Those five tools are enough to change a great many moments because they stop the partner from doing what fear naturally urges: adding more words, more questions, more contact, more interpretation, and more urgency.

Keep the Two Clocks

Remember the two clocks.

Regulation time asks: what can this nervous system do now?

Relationship time asks: what still needs to be discussed, repaired, decided, or changed?

Confusing the clocks creates two opposite harms.

If you force relationship time during severe dysregulation, you add pressure to a system that cannot process it.

If you never return to relationship time, dysregulation becomes a way important issues disappear.

Healthy partnership requires both clocks.

Understanding Is Not Permission

You now have more language for behaviours that once looked baffling.

Use that language to reduce blame where blame is inaccurate.

Do not use it to erase harm.

A meltdown can be involuntary and frightening to witness.

A shutdown can be genuine and painful to wait through.

A flashback can be real and still be triggered by a relationship issue that must be addressed later.

Trauma can explain fear without making all current perceptions accurate.

Autism can explain overload without making all household responsibility optional.

The sentence that holds the book together is:

Compassion changes how we respond; it does not cancel boundaries.

Your Partner Is Not a Problem to Solve

The Moment Map should never turn your loved one into a collection of symptoms.

They are a person with preferences that have nothing to do with autism.

A sense of humour that is not a diagnostic feature.

Bad habits that are simply bad habits.

Talents.

Contradictions.

Political opinions.

Desire.

Boredom.

Kindness.

Selfish moments.

Ordinary anger.

Joy.

Autism matters.

Trauma matters.

Neither should consume personhood.

You Are Not a Supporting Character

The same is true of you.

You are not "the neurotypical partner" in every room.

You are not a treatment environment.

You are not the person whose needs become optional because another person's needs are easier to name clinically.

You are allowed rest.

You are allowed friends.

You are allowed anger.

You are allowed privacy.

You are allowed sexual boundaries.

You are allowed to say no.

You are allowed to need change.

You are allowed to leave a dangerous situation.

You are allowed to decide that love and compatibility are not the same.

Staying connected without losing yourself means the relationship must have room for your nervous system too.

The Final Plan

Complete one final page together if the relationship is safe enough for collaborative planning.

When overload begins, I usually notice:

____

When trauma activation begins, I usually notice:

____

When I lose speech or processing capacity, the best communication method is:

____

In an unclear episode, our default is:

____

Touch during dysregulation is:

always no / ask first / use only this agreed form: ____________________

My return signal is:

____

The safety lines we will not cross are:

____

The unfinished issue after an episode will be revisited by:

____

Professional support we need is:

____

What the supporting partner needs in order not to disappear is:

____

One thing we still enjoy together and will protect is:

____

That last line belongs on the page.

A relationship cannot be built only around what goes wrong.

The Next Moment

The next difficult moment may still be difficult.

Your partner may stop speaking.

A voice may rise.

A reminder may pull the past into the room.

You may feel the familiar urge to fix everything immediately.

This time, you have another option.

Check safety.

Reduce pressure.

Watch capacity.

Choose the protocol.

Let the nervous system come back.

Then return to the relationship.

Not as clinician and patient.

Not as rescuer and problem.

As two adults trying to create enough safety for love to remain love.

References

Andrzejewski, T., Gomez Batista, S., Abu-Ramadan, T., Breitenfeldt, K. E., Tassone, A. U., Winch, A., Rozek, D. C., & McDonnell, C. G. (2024). Examining rates of traumatic events and posttraumatic stress disorder symptoms among autistic adults. *Autism in Adulthood, 6*(3), 374-387. https://doi.org/10.1089/aut.2023.0022

Bargiela, S., Steward, R., & Mandy, W. (2016). The experiences of late-diagnosed women with autism spectrum conditions: An investigation of the female autism phenotype. *Journal of Autism and Developmental Disorders, 46*, 3281-3294. https://doi.org/10.1007/s10803-016-2872-8

Fisher, N., van Diest, C., Leoni, M., & Spain, D. (2023). Using EMDR with autistic individuals: A Delphi survey with EMDR therapists. *Autism, 27*(1), 43-53. https://doi.org/10.1177/13623613221080254

Hull, L., Petrides, K. V., Allison, C., Smith, P., Baron-Cohen, S., Lai, M.-C., & Mandy, W. (2017). "Putting on my best normal": Social camouflaging in adults with autism spectrum conditions. *Journal of Autism and Developmental Disorders, 47*, 2519-2534. https://doi.org/10.1007/s10803-017-3166-5

Jones, D. R., Botha, M., Ackerman, R. A., King, K., & Sasson, N. J. (2024). Non-autistic observers both detect and demonstrate the double empathy problem when evaluating interactions between autistic and non-autistic adults. *Autism, 28*. https://doi.org/10.1177/13623613231219743

Kildahl, A. N., & Helverschou, S. B. (2024). Post-traumatic stress disorder and experiences involving violence or sexual abuse in a clinical sample of autistic adults with intellectual disabilities: Prevalence and clinical correlates. *Autism, 28*(5), 1075-1089. https://doi.org/10.1177/13623613231190948

Kinnaird, E., Stewart, C., & Tchanturia, K. (2019). Investigating alexithymia in autism: A systematic review and meta-analysis. *European Psychiatry, 55*, 80-89. https://doi.org/10.1016/j.eurpsy.2018.09.004

Leicestershire Partnership NHS Trust. (n.d.). *Understanding autistic meltdowns and shutdowns*. https://www.leicspart.nhs.uk/autism-space/health-and-lifestyle/meltdowns-and-shutdowns/

Miller, D., Rees, J., & Pearson, A. (2021). "Masking is life": Experiences of masking in autistic and nonautistic adults. *Autism in Adulthood, 3*(4), 330-338. https://doi.org/10.1089/aut.2020.0083

National Autistic Society. (2020). *Meltdowns: A guide for all audiences*. https://www.autism.org.uk/advice-and-guidance/behaviour/meltdowns/all-audiences

National Institute for Health and Care Excellence. (2018). *Post-traumatic stress disorder (NG116)*. https://www.nice.org.uk/guidance/ng116

Raymaker, D. M., Teo, A. R., Steckler, N. A., Lentz, B., Scharer, M., Delos Santos, A., Kapp, S. K., Hunter, M., Joyce, A., & Nicolaidis, C. (2020). "Having all of your internal resources exhausted beyond measure and being left with no clean-up crew": Defining autistic burnout. *Autism in Adulthood, 2*(2), 132-143. https://doi.org/10.1089/aut.2019.0079

U.S. Department of Veterans Affairs, National Center for PTSD. (n.d.-a). *Coping with traumatic stress reactions*. https://www.ptsd.va.gov/gethelp/coping_stress_reactions.asp

U.S. Department of Veterans Affairs, National Center for PTSD. (n.d.-b). *PTSD treatment basics*. https://www.ptsd.va.gov/understand_tx/tx_basics.asp

U.S. Department of Veterans Affairs, National Center for PTSD. (n.d.-c). *PTSD and the family*. https://www.ptsd.va.gov/professional/treat/specific/ptsd_family.asp

U.S. Department of Veterans Affairs, National Center for PTSD. (n.d.-d). *How does PTSD affect families?* https://www.ptsd.va.gov/family/effect_families.asp

World Health Organization. (2024a). *Clinical descriptions and diagnostic requirements for ICD-11 mental, behavioural and neurodevelopmental disorders*. World Health Organization. https://www.who.int/publications/i/item/9789240077263

World Health Organization. (2024b). *Post-traumatic stress disorder*. https://www.who.int/news-room/fact-sheets/detail/post-traumatic-stress-disorder

www.ingramcontent.com/pod-product-compliance
Lightning Source LLC
LaVergne TN
LVHW050818061126
851857LV00012B/869
* 9 7 9 8 9 0 6 7 8 2 0 6 9 *